INDIAN MYTHOLOGY AND PHILOSOPHY

THE VEDAS, UPANISHADS, BHAGAVAD GITA, KAMA SUTRA… AND HOW THEY FIT TOGETHER

ANCIENT WISDOM
BOOK 4

NEEL BURTON

ACHERON PRESS

When a man knows the best and the greatest,
he becomes the best and the greatest.

— CHANDOGYA UPANISHAD 5.1.1

ABOUT THE AUTHOR

Dr Neel Burton FRSA is a psychiatrist, philosopher, and wine-lover who lives and teaches in Oxford, England. He is a Fellow of Green-Templeton College in the University of Oxford, and the winner of several book prizes including, the feather in his cap, a Best in the World Gourmand Award. His work often features in the likes of *Aeon* and *Psychology Today* and has been translated into several languages. When he is not reading or writing, or imbibing, he enjoys cooking, gardening, learning languages, visiting museums and gardens, and travelling, most of all to sunny wine regions.

Find out more: www.neelburton.com

ALSO BY NEEL BURTON

In the Ancient Wisdom series

Revel in the wisdom of the Ancients

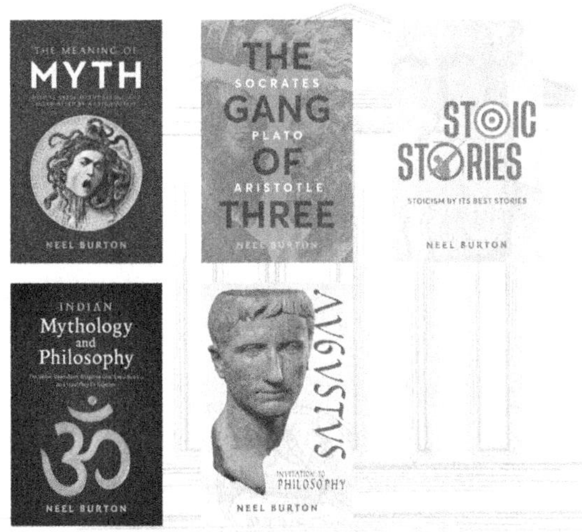

The Meaning of Myth

The Gang of Three: Socrates, Plato, Aristotle

Stoic Stories: Stoicism by its Best Stories

Indian Mythology and Philosophy

Augustus: Invitation to Philosophy

In the Ataraxia series

Begin your journey to peace and power of mind

The Meaning of Madness

Hide and Seek: The Psychology of Self-Deception

Heaven and Hell: The Psychology of the Emotions

For Better For Worse: Essays on Sex, Love, Marriage, and More

Hypersanity: Thinking Beyond Thinking

The Art of Failure: The Anti Self-Help Guide

ANCIENT WISDOM SERIES INTRODUCTION

To be ignorant of the past is to be forever a child. For what is the time of man, lest it be interwoven with that memory of ancient things of a superior age?

— CICERO

The first three books in the Ancient Wisdom series survey a thousand years of Western intellectual history, from the rise of the Greek city states to the peak height of the Roman Empire. This uniquely fertile period, which encompasses the Golden Age of Athens, began in mystical, mythological thought, and culminated in the hyper-rational, hyper-practical philosophy of the Stoics.

The incipient Christian religion absorbed and adapted, and for a long time occulted, many ancient doctrines, which is why, despite their remoteness, they can seem so strangely familiar. In the late Middle Ages, the rediscovery of Plato fuelled the humanistic Renaissance, which pushed back against the Church of Rome.

The Renaissance was a time of great hope and optimism, which, in many ways, proved premature. Faith provides a compelling reason to live, and a compelling reason to be good, which, for better or worse, many people have lost. For all our progress in science, technology, and education, more than one in five adults are now suffering from some form of depression. It's almost as if we've come full circle, minus the philosophy.

Might it then be time to look afresh at these ancient ideas and find in them a happier way of living? Might it be time, in other words, for a new Renaissance?

INDIAN MYTHOLOGY AND PHILOSOPHY

CONTENTS

ABOUT THE BOOK COVER

The Sanskrit ligature on the book cover stands for the sacred sound Om or Aum, which may be chanted before a mantra or during meditation. It is often found at the beginning and end of sacred Hindu texts, and has many names, including the *pranava* ['fore-sound'] and *udgitha* ['chant', 'cosmic song'].

In Indian thought, from the earliest times, there is this notion that the word abstracts from the object, and that Brahman or God, being the ultimate abstraction, abstracts from the word:

> The source of all names is the word, for it is by the word that all names are spoken. The word is behind all names, even as Brahman is behind the word. The source of all forms is the eye, for it is by the eye that all forms are seen. The eye is behind all forms, even as Brahman is behind the eye.
>
> — GREAT FOREST UPANISHAD, I.6

Language, therefore, is the link between man and God.

A similar idea can be found in the Bible, at John 1:1, where it is hard to miss:

> In the Beginning was the word [Greek, *logos*], and the word was with God, and the word was God.

It can also be found in Plato, for example, in Book 6 of the *Republic*, when Socrates says:

> Just as it is by the light of the sun that the visible is made apparent to the eye, so it is by the light of truth and being that the nature of reality is made apparent to the soul.

In one of Æsop's fables, *Zeus, The Animals, and Man*, Zeus, having created the animals, equips each one with its proper qualities, distributing strength to some, speed to others, and wings, fangs, claws, poisons, pelts, hooves, and horns—leaving man to lament that he has received nothing.

Zeus replies:

> On the contrary, you have received the greatest gift of all, for I have given you the word, which, like immortality, is an attribute of the gods. It is mightier than the lion's roar, swifter than the horse's hooves, and can carry you, and your children, higher than the eagle's wings. And if you wield it well, it will far outlive your gravestone.

Like the Ancient Egyptians, the Aryans (or people of the Vedas) believed that the word had a magical or ritual power which complemented its meaning—a view of language that we still retain when we speak of 'spelling' a word. Even away from the sacrificial fire, at work or at home, or in love, words have no effect (or some other effect) if they are not the right ones.

If they had told us at school that we were learning magic, we would have paid a lot more attention.

All day, every day, we are casting spells without even knowing it, abusing the word and weighing down our souls.

By the time of the earliest Upanishads (c. 7th century BCE), Om—possibly derived from the Sanskrit for 'yes'—had become the quintessential word: a cosmic sound and mantra that invoked consciousness, reality, and Brahman or Oneness.

The very long Chandogya Upanishad opens with:

> Om is the closest word to Brahman. Recite this Om as if you are worshipping Brahman ... speech is the essence of human beings; the Rig Veda is the essence of speech; the Sama Veda is the essence of the Rig Veda; and the udghita is the essence of the Sama Veda.

In the Mundaka Upanishad, Om is compared to an archer's bow, by which Atman (the Self) is able to reach its target of Brahman. Only by the focused mind or undistracted person is Brahman to be penetrated.

PREFACE

Sitting down with the *Bhagavad Gita* at the age of sixteen opened many new channels in my mind. Ever since, for the best part of thirty years, I have been searching for a book on Indian thought that ties it all up, coherently and succinctly. Write the book you want to read, they say—and this, here, is it.

Indian thought is complex and contradictory, making it hard to research and write about. There is a staggering amount of material to sift through. There are not one but four Vedas, each with four layers, and, within each layer, several commentaries written over several centuries. The *Mahabharata*, the longest poem in the world, has six times as many lines as the Bible, and four times as many lines as the other major Indian epic, the *Ramayana*—and exists in multiple regional versions. And then there are the Vedangas, the Shastras, the Puranas, the Tantras, and the extensive literature of the philosophical schools... Almost every position, including atomism and hedonism, has been defended by someone at some time. Like much of Western philosophy, much of Indian philosophy is rather sterile and sectarian, and I'll do my best to spare you the detail.

Indian philosophy, unlike its Greek counterpart, is usually pursued within a religious context, with no clear divide between philosophy and theology. The central problem is the nature of the Self, or *Atman*, and its relation to the Absolute, or *Brahman*. On this basis, Indian philosophy is divided into schools, or *darshanas* ['visions'], rather than into branches such as epistemology and metaphysics. That said, Hinduism is a lot looser than the Abrahamic religions, with no founding prophet, no single scripture, no central authority, no core doctrine or code of conduct, and no clear concept of God. Hindus might coherently think of themselves as monotheists, polytheists, pantheists, deists, agnostics, or anything in between. India is a world unto itself: as a religion, Hinduism developed more as a negative concept of contradistinction, and it might be said that Hindus are only Hindus insofar as they are not anything else.

The Buddha explicitly rejected a creator God, yet Buddhism is counted as the fourth largest world religion after Christianity, Islam, and Hinduism—suggesting that the hallmark of religion is not a belief in a creator God, or any god, but a belief in the conservation of values, that is, in something like *karma*, about which the Indian religions, especially Jainism, have a great deal to say. Karma is the greatest constant in Indian thought, lending a family resemblance to Hinduism, Buddhism, and Jainism. Gandhi, for one, regarded Buddhism and Jainism as traditions of Hinduism, which has adaptively assimilated the Buddha as the ninth avatar of Vishnu, after Rama and Krishna, and before Kalki, who will preside over the apocalypse. In Hindu thought, the universe has a moral order that is independent of the gods, who are less than omnipotent. In the Chandogya Upanishad, Indra, the king of the gods, is made to wait 101 years before being told the secret to the self—not a bad deal, considering. Towards the end of the *Mahabharata*, Krishna is killed by a hunter who mistakes him for a deer.

Hindu cosmology is on a colossal scale. The universe contains not one world but thousands of millions. According to the Puranas, Vishnu's ten avatars span a cyclic age, or *maha yuga*, which is 4.32 million years long. A thousand such cycles amount to a single day of Brahma, or *kalpa*, which is 4.32 billion years long, and followed by an equally long night. At the dawn of each kalpa, Brahma re-emerges from a lotus that has stemmed from the navel of Vishnu. A god lives for an entire kalpa but does not survive its dissolution. The Rig Vedic Hymn of Creation [*Nasadiya Sukta*] begins like the Book of Genesis with darkness and water, before candidly abandoning course:

> How then did this creation arise? The gods came after, with the creation of the universe. Who then knows where it came from? Where it came from—perhaps it formed itself, or perhaps it did not—the one who looks down on it, in the highest heaven, he only knows—or perhaps he does not.

Hinduism has been called *Sanatana Dharma*, 'Eternal Order', without beginning nor end. Unlike Christianity and Islam, it arose out of a long process of evolution that began in pre-literate mythical-ritualistic-sacrificial times. From the first Upanishads (c. 800-600 BCE), the Vedic religion became much more introspective-speculative-philosophical, with a monkish, although still elitist, emphasis on renunciation and liberation that, not coincidentally, matched with Buddhism and Jainism. In the *Bhagavad Gita*, composed several centuries later (it is not clear exactly when), Krishna makes a strong case for devotional theism, which is the form assumed by modern, popular Hinduism—epitomized in the West by the Hare Krishnas. Contemporary Indians know little of the older, deeper layers of their culture, of the Vedas and Upanishads, just like Westerners know little, if anything, of Homer, Plato, and Cicero.

Coming to Indian philosophy after having written three books on Greek philosophy, I have been struck by the parallels, and eager to point them out. This book's very epigraph, from the Chandogya Upanishad, echoes Plato in the *Protagoras*: when asked about the food of the soul, Socrates replies, 'Surely, knowledge is the food of the soul.' One is tempted to ask: are the similarities between Greek and Indian thought the result of direct or indirect communication, or are they the result of a common source or common grammar? Or are they rather a universal product of the human mind?

For all the similarities, the Indian way is another way of doing philosophy and arriving at the same insoluble problems, like the problem of evil and the problem of free will. The Indian way is another way of being human, another way of being alive, and a great complement to the Greek or Western way.

I say: elephants as well as horses for the armoury of the mind.

A note on translations: For the Rig Veda, I have generally favoured Wendy Doniger; for the Upanishads and *Bhagavad Gita*, Juan Mascaró.

A note on conventions: Because the Bible and its books are not italicized, I have not italicised Indian revealed scripture, for example, the Rig Veda or Mandukya Upanishad. I drew the line at the *Bhagavad Gita*, which is classed, albeit controversially, as a remembered text.

INTRODUCTION: A PICTURE OF INDIA

If Hinduism has been called *Sanatana Dharma* [Eternal Order] by Hindu nationalists, this is in part because the words 'Hindi' and 'Hindu' are not, in fact, Indian.

The Sanskrit name for the Indus River is *Sindhu*, whence Sindh, the southern-eastern province of modern Pakistan. When borrowing from Sanskrit, the Persians had a habit of changing the initial 's' to an aspirate 'h'. Thus, 'Hindu' was how the Persians came to refer to the people who inhabited the basin of the Indus—which, after appending their region or country suffix, 'stan', they came to call 'Hindustan'.

In his remarkable memoirs, the *Baburnama*, written in a highly Persianized form of Chagatai, the conquering Mughal emperor Babur (d. 1530) states that:

> Most of the inhabitants of Hindustan are pagans [i.e. non-Muslims]; they call a pagan a Hindu. Most Hindus believe in the transmigration of souls. All artisans, wage-earners, and officials are Hindus.

The Greeks, from the time of Herodotus, dropped the 'h' and substituted their own region or country suffix, giving us 'India'. When the British arrived, they gradually restricted the term 'Hindoo' to those Indians who did not identify as Muslim, Sikh, Jain, or Christian, so that, in academic circles, 'Hindu' came to be associated with high-caste Brahmanas [brahmins, or priests] and the Brahmanism derived from the ancient Vedic religion.

In 2023, invitations issued by the President of India to delegates of the G20 referred to him as the 'President of Bharat', 'Bharat' being a Sanskrit name that is used interchangeably with 'India'. Article 1 of the Constitution of India, ratified in 1949, declares: 'India, that is Bharat, shall be a Union of States.' The name 'Bharat' evokes the legendary emperor Bharata, who is regarded as the ancestor of the Bharatas, a prominent tribe mentioned in the Rig Veda, and of the Pandavas and Kauravas, the warring cousins of the *Mahabharata*. It also evokes the Puranas, in which the subcontinent is occasionally referred to as Bharatavarsha, after another Bharata, son of Rishabha.

The *Baburnama* makes for mixed reading. Babur, descended from Tamerlane on his father's side and Genghis Khan on his mother's side ('Mughal' is Persian for Mongol), confesses his bashful lovesickness for a slave boy, Baburi, whom he rescues from a camp-bazaar in Uzbekistan.

> I discovered in myself a strange inclination, nay! as the verse says, 'I maddened and afflicted myself' for a boy in the camp-bazaar, his very name, Bāburī, fitting in ... At that time I composed Persian couplets, one or two at a time; this is one of them: *May none be as I, humbled and wretched and love-sick: No beloved as thou art to me, cruel and careless.*

After losing Samarkand for a third time, Babur, by then emir of Kabul, turns his attention to India. He describes the decisive First Battle of Panipat (1526) against the Sultan of Delhi, Ibrahim Lodi, who, for all his men and elephants, lacked the decisive advantage of gunpowder, which Babur introduced into India. Within a year, Babur would defeat the assembled Rajput Confederation led by Rana Sanga, King of Mewar.

Besides boys, Babur loves wine, fruits, and gardens. After raising a tower of skulls in one line, he discusses a wine-party in the next: 'There was a wine-party in Khawaka Kalan's house, several goatskins of wine having been brought.' When describing a place, he often reports on its grapes and melons, and one day even organizes a melon tasting:

> [The melons of Akhsi] are excellent; they call one kind Mir Timuri; whether in the world there is another to equal it is not known. The melons of Bukhara are famous; when I took Samarkand, I had some brought from there and some from Akhsi; they were cut up at an entertainment and nothing from Bukhara compared with those from Akhsi.

Upon beholding India for the first time, Babur had been taken, and not just by its fabulous wealth:

> It was in the month of Sha'ban [Sha'ban 910 AH, that is, January 1505 CE], the Sun being in Aquarius, that we rode out of Kabul for Hindustan. We took the road by Badam-chashma and Jagdalik and reached Adinapur in six marches. Till that time I had never seen a hot country or the Hindustan border-land. In Ningnahar another world came to view—other grasses, other trees, other animals, other birds, and other manners and customs of clan and horde. We were amazed, and truly there was ground for amaze.

But later, he pines for Kabul, where he asked to be buried:

> Hindustan is a place of little charm. There is no beauty in its people, no graceful social intercourse, no poetic talent or understanding, no etiquette, nobility, or manliness. The arts and crafts have no harmony or symmetry. There are no good horses, meat, grapes, melons, or other fruit. There is no ice, cold water, good food or bread in the markets. There are no baths and no madrasas [colleges]. There are no candles, torches, or candlesticks.

Babur's grandson Akbar extended the empire over most of the subcontinent, and Akbar's grandson Shah Jahan built the Taj Mahal of Agra and Red Fort and Jama Masjid of Delhi.

Another endonym [native name] for India, older even than Bharata, and still occasionally used in certain Southeast Asian countries, is Jambudvipa.

According to Puranic cosmography (individual accounts vary), the world consists of seven concentric continents separated by seven encircling oceans, each double the size of the preceding one. From inner to outer, the seven oceans consist of brine, molasses, wine, ghee, milk, curds, and freshwater. The largest, outermost ocean, of freshwater, is bounded by a mountain range called Lokaloka ['World-no-world'].

The innermost continent in this scheme is Jambudvipa, named for the jambu tree, the delicious berry of which is shaped like India. In the centre is the golden Mount Meru, the abode of the gods, from which four subcontinents spread out like lotus petals. The southern petal corresponds to Bharatavarsha, and the foothills of Mount Meru to the Himalayas (Figure 1).

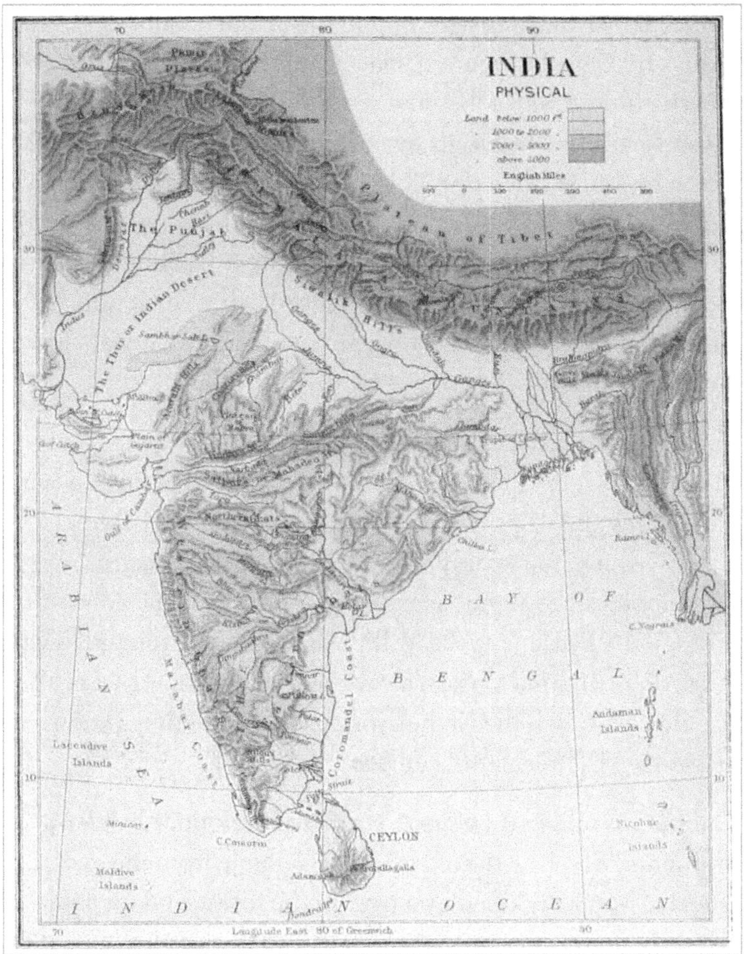

Figure 1. Physical geography of India.
The sub-continent resembles a rose apple (jambu) or lotus petal.

Below, there are seven hells, and above, seven heavens, the highest heaven being Brahmaloka or Brahmapuri, the City of Brahma. Other Puranas detail 28 hells, before stating that there are, in fact, hundreds and thousands.

India's first civilizations grew up in the fertile floodplains of the Indus and Ganges (Figure 1). Place names in the Vedas suggest that the Indo-Aryan tribes first settled in the Sapta Sindhu, or Seven Rivers (the Indus, its five tributaries, and the Saraswati, which has since dried up). This is the same area, roughly, that had been occupied by the Indus Valley Civilization (Chapter 1), one of the early cradles of civilization. The five tributaries of the Indus, which gave the Punjab ['Five Waters', or, to the Greeks, Pentapotamia] its name, are the Jhelum, Chenab, Ravi, Sutlej, and Beas.

The Indo-Aryan tribes gradually spread east along the Doab ['Two Rivers'], the then densely forested alluvial plain between the Ganges and its principal tributary, the Yamuna ['Twin Sister'], which flows parallel to the Ganges. The Ganges, worshipped since Vedic times as the goddess Ganga, flows through the heavens as the Milky Way, and was brought down to Earth by Brahma to wash away the sins of man. As Ganga also flows through the Netherworld, she is sometimes known as Tripathaga ['Three paths, courses, or worlds'].

The story is told in the *Skanda Purana* of the sinner Vahika, a Brahmana who was 'devoid of even a syllable from the Vedas'. One day, Vahika is killed by a tiger in the forest, and his soul arrives before Yama, the god of death and justice also known as Dharmaraja. As he is being prodded with irons, Chitragupta ['Rich in Secrets'], the registrar of the dead, enumerates his many sins, including kicking his mother and killing a cow. Yama sentences him to a kalpa in various hells, and he is dragged away in chains. Meanwhile, aboveground, Vahika's corpse is being torn apart by vultures. A vulture carries off one of his legs but, in the sky, clashes with another bird of prey and drops the ankle bone into the Ganges. For just this, a celestial chariot rescues Vahika and bears him up to heaven.

The third major river system of the north is the Brahmaputra ['Son of Brahma'], which, after merging with the Ganges in the Ganges-Brahmaputra Delta, empties into the Bay of Bengal. This delta is the largest in the world, and the part that is in Bangladesh amounts to some four-fifths of that country's area. All three river systems, the Indus, Ganges, and Brahmaputra, originate in a small area of southwestern Tibet near the picturesque peak of Mount Kailash, which is said to be the abode of Shiva, Parvati, and their sons Ganesha and Kartikeya.

According to the *Bhagavata Purana*, the mountains came into being after Vishnu saved the Earth from the *asura* [anti-god, demon] Hiranyaksha, and hugged it hard.

Ancient texts refer to the Vindhya Mountains as the southern boundary of Aryavarta, the territory of the Indo-Aryan tribes and kingdoms. Still today, the Vindhyas divide the northern plains from southern India. Although of sandstone, they once competed with Mount Meru, growing so tall as to obstruct the sun. Agastya asked them to stoop down so that he could carry the Vedas to Dravidian lands. In reverence for the sage, they bowed deeply, and promised to remain prostrate until he returned. Since Agastya never returned, the Vindhyas remain low. Nevertheless, crossing them was still perilous, owing to thick forests and hostile tribes. In the foothills of the Vindhyas, the Rock Shelters of Bhimbetka contain the earliest known rock art in India. The oldest paintings, on hunter-gatherer themes that include elephants and rhinoceros, have been dated to around 8,000 BCE. Expressions of spirituality on the cave walls still find an echo in local customs, suggesting that aspects of Hinduism may be rooted in prehistoric religion. Running parallel to the Vindhyas is the Narmada ('Jester'), a rift river that carries linga-shaped pebbles known as *banalinga*—and that is therefore sacred to Shiva.

The Vindhyas are one of only two mountain ranges mentioned in the *Jana Gana Mana*, or national anthem of India: '[Thy name] echoes in the hills of the Vindhyas and Himalayas, mingles in the music of the Yamuna and Ganges...' The anthem was originally composed in Bengali by India's first Nobel laureate Rabindranath Tagore (d. 1941), who also composed the national anthem of Bangladesh and inspired that of Sri Lanka.

The Indian subcontinent is surrounded by deep ocean on three sides and high mountains on the fourth. The Chinese monk Fa'hsien (d. 422 CE), in search of Buddhist manuscripts, described crossing the Pamirs into India:

> The mountain itself was just one sheer wall of rock 8,000 feet high, and as one approached it, one became dizzy. If one wished to advance, there was no place for him to place his feet. Below was the Indus River. In former times people had chiselled a path out of the rocks and distributed on the face of the cliff over seven hundred ladders for the descent.

For all that, India's defences are not impregnable, and have been breached at the Khyber Pass, near the modern Pakistan-Afghan border, by, among others, Cyrus the Great, Darius the Great, Alexander the Great, Mahmud of Ghazna, Genghis Khan, Tamerlane, and Babur. The British used the Khyber Pass in the other direction during the Anglo-Afghan Wars. During the Second World War, they erected concrete dragon's teeth on the valley floor for fear of a German tank invasion of India.

The pre-Partition phrase 'Khyber to Kanyakumari' to connote the length of India has since been adapted to 'Kashmir to Kanyakumari'. In fact, the subcontinent has never been unified under one administration. India's three great empires (Maurya, Gupta, and Mughal) never controlled the entire subcontinent, and the British never colonized Nepal and Bhutan.

Today, the subcontinent is divided into five nations: India, Pakistan, Bangladesh, Nepal, and Bhutan, with a combined population of around 1.8 billion. India alone has 22 official languages, and hundreds of unofficial ones—including some five hundred tribal languages.

Much of the subcontinent is hot and humid. The southwest monsoon, from June to September, delivers, or dumps, close to four-fifths of India's annual rainfall. The mould and insects do not lend themselves to the preservation of ancient artefacts and manuscripts, which, owing to the taboo surrounding animal products, are palm leaf rather than the more durable vellum. Once trimmed and cured, rectangular sheets were inscribed with a stylus. A colouring, often based on soot or turmeric, was then applied to the surface and wiped off, to highlight the incised grooves. Each sheet had one or two holes, so that multiple sheets could be bound between boards like a book. Even if stored with insect-repelling herbs, and rubbed with the likes of camphor or lemongrass oil, manuscripts often needed recopying, invariably by a high-caste male, commissioned by an even higher caste male.

The southern counterpart of the Khyber Pass is the Bolan Pass, in Balochistan. Very near to the Bolan Pass is the site of Mehrgarh, exposed in the 1970s by a flash flood. At Mehrgarh, archaeologists have unearthed the earliest evidence of farming and herding in South Asia, going as far back as the aceramic [without pottery] Mehrgarh Period I, which spans the years from around 7000 to 5500 BCE. By 2500 BCE, Mehrgarh and Balochistan had fallen within the ambit of the Indus Valley Civilization, to which we now turn.

1

THE INDUS VALLEY CIVILIZATION

In the mid-1850s, a few years after the British annexation of the Punjab, some railway builders stumbled upon an ancient mound of terracotta bricks at Harappa, in the valley of the Ravi. Despite reports of their antiquity, they carted off the bricks for track ballast, to support nearly 100 miles of railway between Multan and Lahore.

In 1920, John Marshall, the distinguished director of the Archaeological Survey of India (ASI), ordered a full excavation of the site. At around that time, he heard of another site some 400 miles to the south which locals referred to as Mohenjo-daro ['The Mound of the Dead'] after the human and animal bones that lay strewn among the artefacts. Initial digs at Mohenjo-daro uncovered striking similarities between the two sites, and it became apparent that they belonged to an ancient civilization that pushed back the history of India by several thousand years.

In an article for the 24 September 1924 issue of the *Illustrated London News*, Marshall wrote:

> Not often has it been given to archaeologists, as it was given to Schliemann at Tiryns and Mycenæ, or to Stein in the deserts of Turkestan, to light upon the remains of a long forgotten civilisation. It looks, however, at this moment, as if we were on the threshold of such a discovery in the plains of the Indus.

Around a thousand sites have since been reported, including five major urban centres (Harappa, Mohenjo-Daro, and three more). The territory, which straddled the modern India-Pakistan border, stretched some 900 miles along the banks of the Indus and its tributaries, covering an area larger than that of Ancient Egypt and Ancient Mesopotamia combined. The Indus Valley Civilization (IVC), or Harappan Civilization, as it came to be called, also had extensive terrestrial and maritime trade connections with Central Asia, Mesopotamia, and the Arabian Peninsula, among others.

Early centres were populated from Neolithic settlements such as Mehrgahr in Balochistan. Like the valley of the Nile and the basin of the Tigris-Euphrates, the Indus Valley is a semi-arid floodplain with fertile, irrigated land that did not need much clearing. The advent of settled agriculture in such a place led to a food surplus that supported population growth and urban development. At their height, Harappa and Mohenjo-daro may each have counted 30-60,000 inhabitants. Although these cities are some four hundred miles apart, their construction is remarkably similar—and remarkably stable, barely altering over the course of a thousand years. The IVC peaked from around 2700 BCE to 1700 BCE, and represents the flowering of the Indian Bronze Age.

For context: in Egypt, the first pyramid, the Step Pyramid of Djoser in the Saqqara necropolis, dates from c. 2650 BCE; in Europe, the first Cretan palaces, at Knossos, Mallia, and Phaestos, date from a little after c. 2000 BCE.

Rather than growing organically, Harappan settlements were laid out on a similar grid pattern, with communal buildings and the world's earliest sanitation system—a degree of urban planning not to be seen again in the subcontinent until the eighteenth century, when Sawai Raja Jai Singh drew plans for the 'pink city' of Jaipur. Brick houses, some of which were multi-storeyed, opened only to inner courtyards and smaller lanes. Each house had access to covered drains that ran along the main roads, suggesting a fairly egalitarian society. The Harappans also had granaries, dockyards, reservoirs, irrigation canals, and public baths.

But more interesting is what they did not have. First, they did not have palaces or monuments to monarchs. They had citadels but no standing army, with the primary purpose of the citadels, it is thought, being to divert or withstand flood waters. Although the standardization of bricks, road widths, and weights and measures over such an extensive area speaks of a strong central government and efficient bureaucracy, the lack of a monarch and standing army argues against the idea of a conquering empire. Second, they did not have temples, and so, it is inferred, no organized religion. Could this utopia have been the first secular, egalitarian state, or confederation?

Perhaps the most iconic Harappan artefact is a four-inch bronze statuette, 'Dancing Girl', depicting a confident teenager caught in a moment with right hand on hip and left hand on knee (Figure 2). With chin raised, and wearing nothing but bangles and a necklace, she looks much more like a Matisse than anything prehistoric.

In 1947, Sir Mortimer Wheeler, director of the ASI from 1944 to 1948, tentatively attributed the decline and demise of the IVC to a hostile invasion of a light-skinned people from the north, known as the Aryans (Chapter 2).

'It may be no mere chance' he wrote in the ASI bulletin, 'that at a late period of Mohenjo-daro, men, women, and children appear to have been massacred there. On circumstantial evidence, Indra [the Vedic god] stands accused.' But Wheeler had misread the archaeological evidence for the so-called Aryan Invasion Theory. Rather than riding down the mountain in their hordes, the Aryans migrated in pulses and cohabited with the indigenous population.

Instead, the decline of the IVC had to do with climate change, leading to an alteration in the monsoon and the drying up of the Saraswati. Significant silting at sites such as Mohenjo-daro suggests major flooding, which is advanced as a competing theory—echoed, perhaps, in Hindu myths of a primaeval flood (Chapter 16). As is becoming all too clear, droughts and floods can be two faces of the same climate change. Other factors, such as deforestation and turmoil in Mesopotamia, may have contributed to the demise of the IVC.

Of course, it is impossible to write about the Indus Valley Civilization without also writing about its famous seals. These soapstone seals are a little over one inch square, and engraved with an image in the centre and, on top, signs that look like writing. Often, they have a pierced boss on the reverse to accommodate a cord.

The images are most commonly of animals such as bulls, elephants, and rhinoceros. But by far the most represented animal, on over half of the seals, is a 'unicorn' with what seems to be the body of a bull and the head of a zebra, crowned by a single, sigmoidal horn.

Figure 2. The Dancing Girl. Mohenjo-daro, c. 2000 BCE. After Partition, an agreement was reached whereby IVC artefacts would be divided equally between India and Pakistan. India retained the Dancing Girl, while Pakistan received the larger Priest-King.

Some five thousand Indus seals have been found, some as far afield as Central Asia and the Middle East. From the large number of surviving sealings, it seems that they were used like signet rings, pressed into clay or wax to brand wares and sign contracts and receipts. Some seals may also have been worn as amulets or talismans.

Although animals, including bulls, dominate representations on Indus seals and other artefacts, there are no representations of cows. That said, there are some suggestions of continuity with Hinduism. For example, female terracotta figurines have been found with red pigment on the hair parting, similar to the sindoor worn by married Hindu women. Although carved some two thousand years later, the animals on the capital plinths of the pillars of Ashoka (Chapter 14) are of a similar style to those on the Indus seals. The so-called Pashupati ['Lord of animals'] seal, which is more elaborate than most, depicts a cross-legged figure surrounded by animals (Figure 3). Some have interpreted the figure, who has a horned headdress and possibly (it is hard to tell) three heads and a lingam, as an early depiction of Shiva, or proto-Shiva.

If we know relatively little about the IVC, this is in part because the Indus script, like Minoan Linear A, remains undeciphered. It is also because the Harappans had no monarchs, and cremated their dead, so that there are no rich burials like there are in Egypt. The Indus script is the earliest form of writing on the subcontinent, with some inscriptions dating from the early Harappan phase, before 2700 BCE. After the demise of the IVC, writing would not reappear for another millennium.

Thousands of inscriptions have been found, mostly on seals, impressions of seals, and pottery markings. Most are very short, and none is longer than 26 signs. The signs are inscribed from right to left, and occasionally in boustrophedon ['turning ox', alternating right-left, left-right from line to line]. Several hundred signs have been identified, although many are hapax, dis, or tris legomena that occur only once, twice, or thrice. Unless the signs are reducible, their number suggests that the script is logosyllabic, with signs representing words as well as sounds—like Cuneiform, Han characters, and Maya and Aztec glyphs. Certain strokes appear to be numerical.

Figure 3. The Pashupati seal, with surrounding animals and Indus script.

Deciphering the Indus script is difficult for several reasons. First, the inscriptions are short. Second, there are no bilingual or digraphic texts like the Rosetta stone. Third, we have no names, such as the names of cities, kings, or gods. Fourth, the signs might not even represent a language. And fifth, we do not know what that language might be, or even whether it is Indo-European, Dravidian, or something else. Although some Hindu nationalists and Aryan indigenists favour a Sanskritic reading, a lack of affixes and inflections count against it being an Indo-European language—as does an absence or scarcity of horses among the Harappans. The Aryans, to whom we now turn, did not just have horses: they were mad about them.

2

THE ARYANS AND THEIR VEDAS

Before the discovery of the Indus Valley Civilization (IVC), it had seemed as if the sophisticated Indo-Aryans had descended onto a primitive aboriginal population. But after its discovery, it became apparent that the Indo-Aryans were nomadic pastoralists who had migrated into an area once occupied by an advanced urban civilization. This was not the Roman Conquests so much as the Barbarian Invasions, during which Germanic tribes settled in the former territories of the Western Roman Empire.

That the arrival of the Indo-Aryans roughly coincides with the waning of the IVC suggested a hostile invasion, but the exposed skeletons that had excited Mortimer Wheeler turned out to be hasty interments rather than victims of a massacre. Proponents of the Aryan Invasion Theory also seized upon the conflicts mentioned in the Rig Veda, not least a battle fought at Hariyupiyia, which they interpreted as Harappa. But even if its inhabitants did refer to the city as 'Harappa', the Rig Veda makes no mention of a migration, or of the IVC. Today, the Aryan Invasion Theory, involving a fair-skinned people subduing a darker, more backward indigenous population, is seen as wishful thinking on the part of colonisers seeking to legitimize their intrusion into India, the 'jewel in the crown' of the British Empire.

The Indo-Aryans and the closely related Indo-Iranians descended from the Proto-Indo-Iranian culture which had developed on the Eurasian steppes north of the Caspian Sea. The Indo-Aryan migration from these steppes into the Indus Valley began in around 1900 BCE and overlapped with the Late Harappan period (c. 1900-1300 BCE). The nomadic pastoralists who set off from their grassy homeland referred to themselves as *Arya* ['compatriot', and, later, 'noble'], and to their territory in India as *Aryavarta* ['Land of the Arya']. At around the same time, their cousins the Indo-Iranians descended onto the Iranian plateau. In the sacred texts of Zoroastrianism, known as the Avesta, the Ancient Persians speak of themselves as *Airya*, from which derives 'Iran'.

The Indo-Aryans and Indo-Iranians used *Arya* or *Airya* as a cultural and linguistic designation, not a racial one, and other Indo-European peoples never used the term. Perhaps because they believed the highly inflected Sanskrit (Chapter 4) to be the oldest Indo-European language, nineteenth century German philologists such as Max Müller and Friedrich Schlegel took to using 'Aryan' as a catchier synonym for 'Indo-European' or 'Proto-Indo-European'. The term then got taken up and twisted by the Nazis, who began opposing an Aryan 'master race' [*Herrenvolk*] to non-Aryan sub-humans [*Untermensch*]. In Nazi ideology, the tall, blond, blue-eyed Nordic race had remained purely Aryan, while the Aryans on the Asian fringes had degenerated through mixing with foreign races—which is why they had lost their combative vigour and become all dark, meditative, and philosophical. Thus, the original Aryans were no longer Aryan enough.

Figure 4. The Indian swastika, in red.

Still, that did not prevent the Nazis from appropriating the swastika [Sanskrit, *svastika*, 'conducive to well-being'], which Indians (including Hindus, Buddhists, and Jains) continue to use as a symbol of spirituality and auspiciousness (Figure 4). The Nazi *Hakenkreuz* [hooked cross] differs from its inspiration in being black rather than red, in being rotated by 45 degrees, and in omitting the four dots between the four arms. In his autobiographical manifesto, *Mein Kampf* (1925), Adolf Hitler, who once dreamt of being an artist, divulged the tortuous process by which he arrived at a flag for Nazi Germany: 'I myself, meanwhile, after innumerable attempts, have laid down a final form; a flag with a red background, a white disk, and a black hooked cross in the middle. After long trials I also found a definite proportion between the size of the flag and the size of the white disk, as well as the shape and thickness of the hooked cross.' It is high time, I think, to stop referring to the *Hakenkreuz* as a swastika, and return their swastika to the Indians.

For centuries, the Indo-Aryans did not settle down, but roamed around, riding over other people's land and fighting them for cattle. But with the advent of iron, they became increasingly agrarian. In the Later Vedic Period, from the eleventh century BCE, the Aryan heartlands shifted eastwards from the Sapta Sindhu, or Indus Valley, to the Doab, or Gangetic Plain. Tribal units and chiefdoms, called *janas*, each lead by a *rajan* elected by a folk assembly and assisted by a council of elders, began to coalesce into Janapadas [realms or, less commonly, oligarchic republics], including the Vedic heartlands of Kuru and Panchala. By the sixth century BCE, sixteen Mahajanapadas [Great Janapadas], including Kosala, Videha, and Magadha, had been established in a belt running from Gandhara in south-eastern Afghanistan to Anga on the borders of Bengal.

It is said that the Kuru king, Parikshit, and his successor Janamejaya, arranged the Vedic hymns into collections called the Vedas. In the *Mahabharata* (Chapter 20), Parikshit is given as the grandson of the hero Arjuna.

'Veda' derives from the Sanskrit *vid*, 'to know', and ultimately from the Proto-Indo-European *weid*, 'to see'. It is connected to several English words, including: 'advice', 'druid', 'evident', 'guide', 'Hades', 'history', 'idea', 'idol', 'idyll', 'vision', 'visit', and, of course, 'wise'.

In Plato's *Cratylus*, on the philosophy of language, Socrates claims that the god of the underworld is called 'Hades' because he knows [*eidenai*] everything fine and beautiful, and 'Pluto' because he is the source of wealth [*ploutos*]: most people prefer to call him Pluto rather than Hades because they are afraid of what they cannot see [*aeides*].

Vedism, the sacrificial religion of the Indo-Aryans, is related to the Greek, Roman, and Germanic religions. For example, the kingdom of Yama is guarded by two four-eyed dogs, Sharvara and Shyama, reminiscent of Odin's wolves, Geri and Freki, and of Cerberus, the three-headed hound of Hades. The Vedic cognate of Zeus and Jupiter is Dyaus Piter ['Father Sky'], who may appear as a fertilizing bull or as a black horse decked in pearl necklaces. However, most aspects of the Indo-European sky god came to be subsumed by Indra, the chief god, who, like Zeus, overcame his father with the help of his mother.

The most important Vedic gods are personifications of the forces of nature, such as Indra (rain and thunder), Vayu (wind), and Agni (fire). These gods or forces could be controlled or placated by means of ritual sacrifice, or *yajna*. This might have involved the carving up of an animal, or, more often, oblations of butter into a consecrated fire which would flare up in response. The story of the sage Shunahshepa, who, by prayer, saved himself from the fire, suggests that human sacrifice was not unknown.

In time, the Vedic religion came to be influenced by indigenous ideas, not only from the Harappans but also from the Munda peoples to the east, the Dravidian peoples to the south, and the diverse tribal peoples of India, or Adivasis. The Rig Veda, the most archaic layer of the Vedas, orally transmitted since the second millennium BCE, already contains some three hundred non-Indo-European words derived from the Austroasiatic Munda language family and the Dravidian language family.

Despite these interlopers, the Vedas are held to be eternal, and periodically revealed to *rishis* [sages] in visions and voices. Since the mythical Satya Yuga [Age of Truth], they had been orally transmitted from one generation to the next, with, it seems, very little variation or deviation. When writing returned to India, the Vedic hymns were compiled into four collections, the Rig Veda, Yajur Veda, Sama Veda, and Atharva Veda, with considerable overlap between the Rig Veda and the other three. Unlike the Bible, the Vedas are not books so much as musical scores, intended not merely to be read but to be performed, with the experience heightened by the copious consumption of hallucinogenic soma.

Compiled in around 1000 BCE, the Rig Veda ['Knowledge of Praise'] is the longest of the Vedas, with 1028 hymns arranged in ten *mandalas*, or books. The Sama Veda ['Knowledge of Songs'] consists almost entirely of selected verses from the Rig Veda arranged for chanting. The Yajur Veda ['Knowledge of Worship'] is a collection of formulas for sacrificial rituals; unlike the Rig, Sama, and Atharva Vedas, it is mostly prose. The Atharva Veda is named for Atharvan, the rishi who, having brought Agni to life, first gave sacrifice. Because of its emphasis on the preoccupations of ordinary people, including popular spells to counter evil, hardship, and disease, it has been called 'the Veda of everyday life'. The Atharva Veda contains the seeds of Ayurveda, the Indian system of medicine (Chapter 23).

Each of the Vedas contains four parts, or layers: the Samhitas, Brahmanas, Aranyakas, and Upanishads. The Samhitas are the most ancient layer, and consist of hymns, mantras, and prayers. Next come the Brahmanas, which were compiled from around 900 to 700 BCE. The Brahmanas might be regarded as priestly guidebooks, which explain the Samhitas and instruct on the enactment of the connected rituals. They also include legends, histories, and stories. Each Veda has one or more Brahmanas, and each Brahmana is associated with a particular Vedic school or *shakha*. Fewer than twenty Brahmanas are extant. The two extant Brahmanas of the Rig Veda are the Aitareya Brahmana of the Shakala Shakha, and the Kausitaki Brahmana of the Baskala Shakha.

Part incorporated into the Brahmanas are the Aranyakas, or so-called Forest Treatises, to be meditated upon in the solitude of the forest. The Aranyakas, which may contain secret rites for the initiated, tend to be more mystical than the Brahmanas. They mark the transition to the philosophical Upanishads (Chapter 5), and certain Upanishads are embedded within an Aranyaka. For instance, the Aitareya Upanishad is embedded in the second book of the Aitareya Aranyaka, which is itself embedded in the Aitareya Brahmana.

The Rig Veda contains the Gayatri Mantra [3.62.10], known as 'the Mother of the Vedas':

> Let us meditate on that excellent glory of the divine vivifying Sun, may he enlighten our understandings.

Many Hindus, even today, recite the Gayatri at sunrise, preceded by Om and the great mystical utterance, *bhur bhuvah svah*. The Gayatri gave its name to its poetic metre, which, after the Trisubh, is the second most common Rig Vedic metre, making up around a quarter of the Rig Veda. The Gayatri metre consists of 24 syllables in three lines of eight syllables (3 x 8), and the Trisubh of 44 syllables in four lines of eleven syllables (4 x 11). Both the mantra and the metre are personified as the goddess Gayatri.

Among several creation myths in the Rig Veda is the *Purusha Sukta*, or Hymn of the Cosmic Man [10.90], according to which the gods created the universe by sacrificing a cosmic man:

> When they divided the Man, into how many parts did they apportion him? What do they call his mouth, his two arms and thighs and feet? His mouth became the Brahmin; his arms were made into the Warrior, his thighs the People, and from his feet the Servants were born.

The *Purusha Sukta*, which echoes the dismemberment of the giant Ymir in Norse mythology, reinforces the *bandhus*, or bonds, between this world and that of the gods. It is the only hymn to explicitly mention the four *varnas* ['colours', castes], and, for this reason, is thought to have been a later insertion into the Rig Veda.

For a long time, the Indo-Aryans only distinguished between two classes, themselves, the Arya, and the people they overran, the Dasas. The social mobility in the Rig Veda is such that it is perfectly possible for a physician to marry a miller, and for their son to be a poet:

> I am a poet; my dad's a physician, and mum a miller with grinding stones. With diverse thoughts we all strive for wealth, going after it like cattle. O drop of soma, flow for Indra [RV 9.112].

In the Upanishads, Purusha, the cosmic man, becomes more of an abstraction, referred to as Brahman or Paramatman.

Horses feature prominently in the Rig Veda. There is a Hymn to the Horse (1.161, 'You gods fashioned the horse out of the sun...') and even a Requiem for a Horse (10.56, 'You are a victorious racehorse with the power to win victory; go happily to the mares who long for you...').

The grandest of Vedic rituals is the Ashvamedha, or Horse Sacrifice, performed by a triumphant king to consolidate and extend his territorial claims. The Ashvamedha is mentioned in several places and detailed in the Shatapatha Brahmana. In brief, a white stallion with black spots is set to roam freely across neighbouring territories, accompanied by a retinue of the king's finest warriors. For one year, any rival can dispute the king's sovereignty over those lands by challenging the warriors and capturing or killing the horse. After the year is over, the horse is guided back to the capital, where the king undergoes a three-day consecration that culminates in the killing of the horse. The chief queen simulates copulation with the dead horse, after which it is dismembered and sacrificed, with the king assuming the title of *chakravartin* [universal monarch]. At the end of the *Mahabharata*, King Yudhishthira performs a horse sacrifice, with his brother Arjuna escorting the horse in its wanderings across the entire earth. The Ashvamedha was rarely enacted in post-Vedic times; it was last performed in 1741 by Sawai Raja Jai Singh of Jaipur.

The Rig Vedic hymns, although sacred, are never introspective or world-denying, but, on the contrary, celebrate life.

One hymn, The Waters of Life [10.9], begins:

> Waters, you are the ones who bring us the life force. Help us to find nourishment so that we may look upon great joy.

And it ends:

> I have sought the waters today; we have joined with their sap.
> O Agni full of moisture, come and flood me with splendour.

The most resonant Rig Vedic hymns are not at all religious: there is a hymn dedicated to frogs [7.103] that compares their monsoonal croaking to the chanting of Brahmanas; a dialogue between Yama and Yami [10:10] in which the god of death rebuffs his sister's advances; and a lament from a pathological gambler [10.34] who is so deeply indebted that his wife spurns him, and his mother-in-law hates him.

Whereas the Harappans left us many artefacts and no words, the Indo-Aryans left us few artefacts but many words.

3

VEDIC GODS: INDRA, AGNI, SOMA, AND THE REST

Going by number of dedicated hymns, the three most important Rigvedic deities are Indra (250), Agni (200), and Soma (123), followed by the Ashvins, Varuna, and the Maruts.

The mythology of India can seem less consistent than that of Greece. Rather than the work of a single person or even a single period, the Vedas are a centuries-long accretion, and part of a still ongoing tradition. Greek mythology, on the other hand, benefited—if benefited is the word—from being reordered and rationalized by the likes of Homer and Hesiod, whose versions became authoritative if not definitive.

Vishnu and Shiva, who would come to dominate the Hindu pantheon, have only bit parts in the Samhitas, with Shiva then going under the name of Rudra. Just six out of 1028 hymns are dedicated to Vishnu: he is portrayed as a solar god who helps Indra defeat the dragon Vritra. Even fewer hymns are dedicated to Rudra, a volatile and potentially destructive god who, like the figure on the Pashupati seal, is associated with wilderness, retreat, and animals.

In the Aitareya Brahmana [3.33], Prajapati, having created the *devas* [gods], creates earthly beings by metamorphosing into a stag and mating with his daughter, Ushas [Dawn], who had adopted the form of a doe. To punish him for 'doing what is not done', the appalled devas produce Rudra, who returns Prajapati from the path of self-indulgence to the path of self-realization. In this Brahmanic (and therefore relatively late) myth, Prajapati appears to have taken on some of the aspects of Dyaus and Indra, including father-daughter incest.

This idea of creation resulting from an original injustice is also found in Anaximander (d. c. 546 BCE). This fragment from his *On Nature*, preserved in Simplicius (d. c. 540 CE), is the oldest extant piece of Greek philosophical writing:

> The things that are perish into the things out of which they come to be, according to necessity, for they pay the penalty and retribution to each other for their injustice in accordance with the ordering of time, as [Anaximander] says in rather poetical language.

In *Philosophy in the Tragic Age of the Greeks*, Nietzsche, in discussing Anaximander, quotes Schopenhauer in saying that humans 'are really creatures who should not exist and who are doing penance for their lives by their manifold sufferings and their death.' For these pessimists, creation is an aberration, and a distraction from self-realization. This world denial, although alien to the Samhitas, looms large in the Upanishads, which Schopenhauer called 'the production of the highest human wisdom' and 'almost superhuman in conception'.

Prajapati ['Lord of Creation'] is later assimilated with Brahma and other gods, so that the term 'Prajapati' comes to apply to any creator god or sage: in the *Bhagavad Gita*, for example, it is one of the many epithets of Krishna.

Figure 5. Indra riding Airavata, who is more often portrayed with several heads and/or several trunks.

Indra (the etymology of the name is unknown) is the subject of almost a quarter of Rig Vedic hymns. Like Zeus, he wields a thunderbolt [*vajra*], as well as a *chakra* [discus], *jala* [net], and other weapons. And like Zeus, he often strays from the marital bed. But his greatest love is for soma, which gives him the strength required to fight the *asuras* [anti-gods] and lead cattle raids against the Dasas. The dragon Vritra, whom he slays, is a leader of the asuras and personification (or transmogrification) of drought.

Indra is not alone in these feats: he has his *vahana* [mount], the elephant Airavata (Figure 5), and various allies, including Vayu, god of the winds and herald of the gods, and the Maruts. The Maruts are a troop of violent storm gods who follow in the train of Indra. At times regarded as the sons of Rudra, they are later transferred into the train of Shiva.

The net of Indra, or *Indrajala*, can stand for *maya* [illusion], and, by extension, for all of creation. But over the centuries, Indra is replaced at the head of the Hindu pantheon by the *Trimurti* ['three forms'], Brahma the creator, Vishnu the maintainer, and Shiva the destroyer, who, in later stories, set out to humble Indra and demonstrate their superiority.

Already in the Chandogya Upanishad (c. seventh century BCE), Indra has been reduced to a mere seeker after wisdom. He and his nemesis Virochana, king of the asuras, go to Prajapati's ashram to learn the secret of the *Atman* [the Self]. Prajapati takes them both in, and, after 32 years, summons them and tells them that Atman is the reflection of the self in the pupil of the eye. Satisfied with this answer, Virochana returns to the asuras, who take to venerating the bodily self.

But Indra is not so sure, and goes back to the ashram. After 32 more years as a *brahmacharya* [celibate student], Prajapati tells him that Atman is the dream self. Still full of doubt, he is made to wait another 32 years, before being told that Atman is the unconscious self. When he protests that no good can come out of this knowledge, Prajapati keeps him for five more years, and, after a total of 101 years, finally tells him the secret of Atman. If Atman is neither the waking self, nor the dreaming self, nor the sleeping self, then what is Atman?

By having Indra wait for what is the natural lifespan of a (wise) man, Prajapati is making the point that the deepest truths cannot simply be taught, but must painstakingly be learnt. Only by much patience and perseverance, which Virochana did not possess, and an orientation to the Platonic form of the Good, is it possible to share in the knowledge of the gods.

But you, dear reader, will only have to wait until Chapter 7 for the secret of the Self.

In another story, this time in the *Brahma Vaivarta Purana* (late first millennium CE), Indra, flush from his victory over Vritra, orders the Indian Dædalus, Vishvakarma, to build him an opulent palace. But enough is never enough, and Indra keeps pressing the architect for something grander. Finally, the fed-up Vishvakarma appeals to Brahma, who in turn appeals to Vishnu and Shiva.

Sometime later, a Brahmin boy arrives at the court of Indra and praises his palace, adding that no previous Indra lived in such splendour, or for that matter, any Indra in any of the infinite worlds. As he speaks, the boy sees a procession of ants crossing before him, and laughs. When Indra asks why he is laughing, he explains that each ant is a former Indra, reincarnated as an ant on account of his pride. At this point, a hermit enters the hall, and explains that each of the hairs on his chest is like an Indra: whenever a hair falls, another replaces it. Because life is so short, he has not troubled to make a living, build a house, or found a family—for of what use would such things be?

The Brahmin boy is Vishnu is disguise, the hermit, Shiva. The humbled Indra releases Vishvakarma and resolves to become a hermit. Concerned about his kingdom, his wife appeals to the rishi Brishaspati, who teaches Indra to tread a line between the worldly and the godly.

Agni—the name is related to 'ignite' and 'igneous'—is the god of fire, especially the sacrificial fire, but also the domestic fire, the fire of the sun, the fire of the eyes, the fire of digestion, and the fire of the funeral pyre. If cremation took precedence over burial among the Indo-Aryans, this is in no small part because of the association between fire and purity, especially ritual purity. Sati, or suttee, the rare, supererogatory practice of a widow immolating herself on her husband's funeral pyre, does not feature in the Vedas, and first appears in the *Mahabharata*.

In 1829, it was outlawed by the British, who pointed to it as a justification for their rule. Agni also lives on in the traditional Hindu wedding, which revolves around a fire-altar: after tying the sacred knot known as the *mangalasutra*, the bride and groom circumambulate the fire seven times, after which their union becomes irrevocable. As the primary recipient of all sacrifices, Agni is second only to Indra in the Vedic pantheon, and features in almost a third of Rig Vedic hymns. Although regarded as the twin brother of Indra, he is also presented, more poetically, as the offspring of a pair of kindling sticks. As an ailing newborn, he required a lot of care, before growing so strong as to devour his parents. Over time, Rudra took over his destructive aspect, leaving him as an unequivocal friend of humanity, protector of the hearth, bringer of civilization, and intermediary of the gods.

To defeat Vritra, Indra 'drank at once three lakes of pressed-out soma' [RV 5.29]. Soma, the elixir of the gods, made both gods and men immortal and invincible:

> We have drunk of the soma; we have become immortal; we have gone to the light; we have found the gods. What can hostility do to us now, and what the malice of a mortal, o immortal one?
>
> — RIG VEDA 8.48

Just as the Greeks elevated wine into a god, Dionysus, so the Indo-Aryans elevated soma into Soma, although soma is perhaps better compared to ambrosia than to wine—and, of course, to the Zoroastrian *haoma*, which may have been the same substance. 'Ambrosia' literally means 'not mortal', as does *amrita*, one of the names for soma, which itself, like haoma, derives from the Indo-Iranian root **sav-*, 'to press'.

One of the Rig Veda's ten mandalas, the Soma Mandala, with 114 hymns, is entirely devoted to soma. Despite this, Soma, especially when compared with Indra, or Dionysus, remains poorly characterized, standing in, in the main, as a synonym for soma. In one myth, a bird of prey, acting for Manu [the first man], steals a stalk of soma from the gods; in another myth, it is Agni, the god of fire, who does the deed, making Agni a kind of Prometheus figure. Thereafter, soma becomes a libation to the gods, poured into the sacrificial fire, with the remainder consumed by the officiants.

The identity of the soma plant remains a matter of contention. Several candidates have been proposed, including *Amanita muscaria* (fly agaric), *Cynanchum acidum* (somalatha), *Ephedra sinica* (ma huang), *Peganum harmala* (wild rue), and various species of *Psilocybin* (magic mushrooms). One hymn, *Soma Pressed in the Bowls*, describes the production process. It seems that, after being soaked in water, the stalks of the soma plant were pressed by stones into a wooden bowl, with the juice then filtered through a woollen sieve before being mixed with the likes of milk, water, and honey. By all accounts, the finished drink, especially when paired with a good hymn, had some considerable expansive properties:

> The two world halves cannot be set against a single wing of mine. Have I not drunk soma? In my vastness, I surpassed the sky and this vast earth. Have I not drunk soma?
>
> — RIG VEDA 10.119

The sky god Varuna preceded Indra, briefly, at the head of the Vedic pantheon. He is the lord of *Rita* [Justice, Order], the precursor of Dharma. From up on high, he watches with a thousand eyes, the stars, over the deeds of man, and punishes those who transgress his opaque moral code, which is never revealed. As king of the asuras, Varuna leads the Adityas, or benevolent asuras, who assist him in his task. After the defeat of Vritra, who led the malevolent asuras, he turned into a deva, while the asuras became associated with demons. In several hymns, Indra himself is described as an asura. According to the Great Forest Upanishad [1.3.1], both the devas and asuras are the sons of Prajapati, and it is only by the Udgitha, that is, by Om, that the devas surpassed the asuras. Varuna is often invoked with Mitra, god of the oath, who also began as an asura, and is later associated with oceans and rivers. His Zoroastrian analogue is Ahura Mazda.

Like other Indo-European horse twins, such as Castor and Pollux (the *Dioskouroi*, or 'boys of Zeus'), the handsome and forever young Ashvins [*asva*, 'horse'] are the helpers of humankind. Like Asclepius and the centaur Chiron, they are physicians to the gods. And like Asclepius and Chiron, they are the sons of the sun, Surya/Apollo. Their twin duality, between light and dark, life and death, is reflected in their association with twilight; each morning, their horse-drawn chariot leads the way for Ushas and Surya.

Unlike the other Vedic gods, Surya retained his place in the later Hindu pantheon, and it is to him that the Gayatri mantra is addressed. In several hymns, he rides in a chariot drawn by seven horses, in the train of his mother Ushas.

But the Aitareya Brahmana (c. seventh century BCE) overturns this poetic portrayal with a stray piece of science:

> The sun causes day and night on earth because of revolution, when there is night here, it is day on the other side, the sun does not really rise or sink.
>
> — AITAREYA BRAHMANA 3.44

4

SANSKRIT AND THE GRAMMAR OF PANINI

In 1771, William Jones published a Persian grammar under the pen name Youns Uksfardi, 'Jones of Oxford'. The 25-year-old polyglot also had the command of Latin, Greek, Hebrew, Arabic, French, Italian, Spanish, Portuguese, and German, as well as his native English and Welsh. Even as a boy at Harrow, his headmaster had been heard to say that Jones had more Greek than him. By the end of his life in 1794, he had a fair competence, or better, in 28 languages, including Chinese.

In 1784, a year after his arrival in India to take up a position of judge in the High Court of Calcutta, Jones—or Sir William, as he now was—founded the 'Asiatick Society' (later, the Asiatic Society) dedicated to 'Oriental research'. When the Brahmanas refused to teach the *mleccha* [outsider], knighted or not, the eternal language of the gods, he found himself a Vaishya teacher at the Nadiya Hindu University.

In February 1786, in his Third Anniversary Discourse to the Asiatick Society, Jones declared:

> The Sanskrit language is of a wonderful structure; more perfect than the Greek, more copious than the Latin, and more exquisitely refined than either, yet bearing to both a stronger affinity ... than could possibly have been produced by accident; so strong indeed, that no philologer could examine all three, without believing them to have sprung from a common source, which, perhaps, no longer exists...

Compare, for example, the Sanskrit *matar*, *pita*, *bhratar*, *svasar* to the English 'mother', 'father', 'brother', 'sister', or the Latin *matar*, *pater*, *frater*, *soror*. Or compare the Sanskrit/Greek cognates *maha/megas* [great], *dama/domos* [house], *kravis/kreas* [meat], *naman/onoma* [name], and *mus/mus* [mouse].

The Indo-European languages began to diverge from a common ancestor in the course of the fourth millennium BCE, in tandem with the Indo-European migrations out of the Pontic-Caspian steppe. The parent language, referred to as Proto-Indo-European (PIE), has largely been reconstructed by the comparative method. PIE had elaborate systems of morphology and phonology with sophisticated features such as inflection (including declension and conjugation), ablaut, and accent. Reconstructed words in PIE are conventionally marked with an asterisk to indicate that they are undocumented, for example, **magh* [to help, to be able, to be powerful], the presumed origin of *maha* and *megas* (and, in English, 'might', 'magician', and 'machine').

The oldest documented Indo-European language is Hittite, from Anatolia, which, however, lacks some of the grammatical features of other early-attested Indo-European languages such as Mycenaean Greek and Vedic Sanskrit. The text in question is a clay tablet inscribed in cuneiform on behalf of a conquering king, Anitta, who reigned in the eighteenth century BCE.

The Suppiluliuma-Shattiwaza Treaty, signed between a Hittite and a Mitanni king in around 1380 BCE, invokes certain gods, four of whom—Indara, Uruvanass, Mitras, and Nasatianna—correspond to the Vedic gods Indra, Varuna, Mitra, and the Nasatyas (an epithet of the Ashvins).

The earliest known inscriptions in Mycenaean Greek, from the 'Room of Chariot Tablets' at Knossos, date from the latter half of the fifteenth century BCE.

The earliest known inscriptions in Sanskrit, in the Brahmi script, date from the second or first century BCE. Among them are the Hathibada Ghosundi Inscriptions in Rajasthan and the Ayodhya Inscription of Dhana in Uttar Pradesh.

Sanskrit is closely related to Avestan (Iranian), which forms part of the same Indo-Iranian subfamily of languages. Already in antiquity, Sanskrit, like Avestan, had a certain cachet as the language of liturgy: implicit in its etymology ['put together', 'perfected', 'refined'] is a comparison with Prakrit ['primordial', 'natural'], the vernacular, or vernaculars, of secular, everyday life. Brahmanas would have needed to be at least bilingual, if only to be scolded by their wives and mothers.

Over the first millennium BCE, Vedic Sanskrit evolved into Classical Sanskrit, the form codified, or petrified, by Panini. Classical Sanskrit is more streamlined: for example, it has dropped the subjunctive and injunctive moods, and has only one way of forming infinitives—compared to as many as twelve in Vedic Sanskrit. On the other hand, noun compounding is much freer than in Vedic Sanskrit (or indeed German), leading to some very long, and creative, word formations. Classical Sanskrit rose into the language of predilection not only for Brahmanas but also for Buddhist and Jain scholars.

In its classical form, Sanskrit is a highly inflected language with three genders (masculine, feminine, neuter), three numbers (singular, dual, plural), and eight cases (nominative, accusative, instrumental, dative, ablative, genitive, locative, and vocative, respectively, for subject, object, method, objective, origin, possession, location, and invocation). Nouns and adjectives are also inflected, so that word order is very flexible. There are three voices (active, middle, passive), four moods (indicative, optative, imperative, conditional), and six tenses, including three for the past and two for the future. Although Sanskrit makes heavy use of the vowel 'a', it is based on long and short syllables rather than stressed syllables, and has more sounds than English. Unlike English, it has no definite or indefinite articles and no present or past continuous. And unlike English, it is highly phonetic: to know the spelling is to know the pronunciation, and vice versa. Even the positional sound changes collectively referred to as *sandhi* are written down to preserve the sacred sound of the spoken, or sung, language.

Today, three out of four Indians have an Indo-European language as their mother tongue, with most of the rest having an unrelated Dravidian language such as Telugu, Tamil, Kannada, or Malayalam. Sanskrit stands in the Constitution of India as both a classical and an official language, with a place akin to that of Latin in the West, as the language of moment.

Sanskrit is usually written in the Devanagari script ['divine script of the city'], which developed from the Gupta script and ultimately from the Brahmi script—from which all Indian and Southeast Asian scripts derive. The oldest indisputably dated full inscriptions in the Brahmi script, in Prakrit, are the Edicts of Ashoka, dating to around 250 BCE. But the earlier emergence of prose texts such as the Brahmanas (900-700 BCE), which would have been hard to conceive without writing technology, suggests that the script predates Ashoka by several centuries.

Figure 6. The word Sanskrit in the Devanagari script.

In regular use by the seventh century CE, Devanagari is also the standard script for well over a hundred languages, including Hindi and Marathi, making it the world's fourth most commonly used writing system, after the Latin alphabet, Chinese characters, and the Arabic alphabet. Devanagari is a left-to-right abugida, or segmental writing system, with 48 primary characters: 34 consonants, 10 vowels, and 4 diphthongs. It is an abugida insofar as a consonant lacking diacritic marks is read as the consonant followed by a short /a/, which can then be altered or muted. The script is recognizable by its vertical bars (full or half) supporting most of the letters, and, above all, by its connected head strokes, called *shirorekha*, from which the letters hang (Figure 6).

The power and position of the Brahmanas stemmed from knowledge, and, more specifically, from knowledge of ritual words and deeds. In a culture of ritual sacrifice, the close connexion between words, deeds, and outcomes reinforced the assumption that to speak correctly is to think and act correctly, and powerfully. Thus, the study of language, and the need to preserve it from 'corruption', became paramount.

In his grammar, the *Astadhyayi*, or *Book of Eight Chapters*, Panini, who lived in the sixth to fifth centuries BCE (his dates are conjectural), cites ten grammarians who went before him. Although his grammar was not the first, it so outshone previous works as to make them redundant.

Written, perhaps, at the University of Taxila, which began, in Gandhara, as a seat of Vedic learning, the *Astadhyayi* lays out the grammatical structure of Sanskrit in 3959 aphoristic remarks, or *sutras*, supplemented by three ancillary texts. In a letter to a colleague, the linguist Leonard Bloomfield (d. 1949) wrote that 'Panini gives the formation of every inflected, compounded, or derived word, with an exact statement of the sound-variations (including accent) and of the meaning.'

The *Astadhyayi* is not merely descriptive but prescriptive and generative, with algebraic or algorithmic rules and metarules governing every aspect of the language. It is regarded as the first ever formal system, predating the syllogistic logic of Aristotle by up to two centuries.

To the compressed sutras, intended to assist memorization and oral dissemination, later grammarians appended elucidatory comments called *vartikka*. Some grammarians wrote entire commentaries called *bhashyas*, to unfold and illustrate the sutras. The most prominent *bhashya* is the *Mahabhashya* [Great Commentary] of Patanjali, composed in the second century BCE. In the *Mahabhashya*, Patanjali also discusses Katyayana's otherwise lost elaboration of Panini, the *Varttikakara*, thereby uniting in a single work India's three greatest grammarians.

Inevitably, all this thinking on grammar led to the beginnings of formal philosophy, as when Patanjali formulates the law of the excluded middle (1.1.44: 'it is impossible for a statement to express simultaneously a rule and a prohibition'), or skirts around the law of double negation [1.5]:

Figure 7. Five-rupee Panini stamp released in August 2004 by the Indian Department of Posts 'in commemoration of India's Heritage in Grammar and Mathematics'.

> Now words have to be examined. How is this to be done? Are (correct) words to be taught, or perhaps incorrect words, or perhaps both? Our purpose will be served by the teaching of either. Thus by a restrictive condition on what food is fit to be eaten is implied a prohibition of what food is not fit to be eaten ... Or, alternatively, by a prohibition of what is not fit to be eaten is implied a restrictive condition on what is fit to be eaten. For example when we say 'the domestic fowl is not fit to be eaten, the domestic pig is not fit to be eaten' it is implied that the wild variety (of these animals) is fit to be eaten.

The *Astadhyayi*, which has been compared to a Turing machine, remains the most complete generative grammar of any language, and set the standard for Classical Sanskrit. According to the *Panchatantra*, Panini was killed by a lion. But as the 'father of linguistics', he lives on not only in his own work but also in that of modern linguists such as Ferdinand de Saussure, who lectured on Sanskrit, and Leonard Bloomfield, who acknowledged him as his role model.

Panini's grammar formed the foundation of Vyakarana, one the six Vedangas, or 'limbs of the Vedas', a set of appendices or assists to the by then arcane and archaic Vedas. The other five Vedangas are on Shiksha (phonetics), Chhandas (metre or prosody), Nirukta (etymology), Kalpa (ritual), and Jyotisha (astronomy and astrology, for timing of rituals).

The founding scholar of Nirukta is Yaska, who is mentioned by Panini. His eponymous *Nirukta* has traditionally been held to include the *Nighantu*, or *Book of Glossary*, which, I think, is the earliest ever thesaurus. Yaska held that nouns, like, say, 'teacher' or 'office' (my examples), ultimately derive from verbs, 'to teach', 'to officiate', with the ontological implication that movement or action precedes essence or form.

The Great Forest Upanishad looks upon the Vedangas as an integral part of the Brahmana layer of Vedic texts, even though the Vedangas probably developed at around the same time as the principal Upanishads.

The Vedangas are not to be confused with Vedanta ['conclusion of the Vedas'], the philosophical school that arose out of the study of the Upanishads. Vedanta, also known as Uttara-Mimamsa, is one of the six *darshanas* ['visions'], or orthodox schools of Hindu philosophy (Chapter 26).

Neither are the Vedangas to be confused with the extensions or applications of the Vedas known as the Upavedas: Ayurveda (medicine), associated with the Atharva Veda; Gandharvaveda (music and dance), associated with the Sama Veda; Dhanurveda (archery and martial arts), associated with the Yajur Veda; and Sthapatyaveda (architecture), associated with the Rig Veda.

And with that, let us turn to the crowning glory of the Vedas: the Upanishads.

5

THE UPANISHADS

The national motto of India, *Satyameva Jayate* [Truth Alone Triumphs], is from the Mundaka Upanishad. It features in the Devanagari script at the base of the State Emblem of India, which is an adaptation of the Lion Capital of Ashoka (Figure 8).

'Upanishad' means something like 'hidden connections', 'secret teaching', or 'esoteric doctrine', literally, 'a sitting at [the feet of the teacher]'. Upanishadic wisdom can only be transmitted to those who are fit to receive it, by those who are fit to teach it. In a line that is repeated in the Mundaka Upanishad, the Katha Upanishad tells us that Atman is reached 'not through the intellect and sacred teaching [but] by the chosen of him—because they choose him. To his chosen the Atman reveals his glory.' According to the oldest of the verse Upanishads, the Kena, Brahman 'comes to the thought of those who know him beyond thought, not to those who imagine he can be attained by thought ... He is known in the ecstasy of an awakening which opens the door of life eternal.'

Although part of the Vedas, the Upanishads tend to take a dim, if diplomatic, view of what went before. 'Of what use' asks the Shvetashvatara Upanishad, 'is the Rig Veda to one who does not know the Spirit from whom the Rig Veda comes?' 'Great is the Gayatri' says the Chandogya Upanishad, 'but how much greater is the infinity of Brahman!' The Brihadaranyaka [Great Forest] Upanishad promises freedom from the very things valued by the Vedas and Vedic society: 'It is when they come to know this self that Brahmanas give up the desire for sons, the desire for wealth, the desire for worlds...' In a passage known as the Udgitha of the Dogs [1.12], the Chandogya satirizes the Brahmanas as a procession of dogs, who chant: 'Om, we will eat! Om, we will drink! ... O Lord of food, bring us food here. Bring us food here. Om.'

By a restrictive definition, there are around 108 Upanishads. The first dozen or so are the most important and referred to as the *mukhya* [main or major] Upanishads. Many 'Upanishads' are much later sectarian texts (Vaishnavite, Shaivite...), claimed as Upanishads to lend them the force of revelation. Although a part of the *Mahabharata*, some look upon the *Bhagavad Gita* (Chapter 21), with some justification, as an Upanishad. No doubt, many Upanishads have been lost.

In the Vedas, there are ten embedded Upanishads, with all ten regarded as *mukhya*. They are the Aitareya (Rig Veda); the Kena and Chandogya (Sama Veda); the Katha, Isha, Great Forest, and Taittiriya (Yajur Veda); and the Prashna, Mundaka, and Mandukya (Atharva Veda). Although embedded in the Vedas, these Upanishads differ from the Brahmanas in language and style, with a shift comparable, in English, to that between Beowulf and Chaucer, or Chaucer and Shakespeare. Also regarded as *mukhya* by some scholars are the heavily commented Kaushitaki, Maitri, and Shvetashvatara. Some of the *mukhya* Upanishads are in mostly prose; others are in verse.

Figure 8. The Lion Capital of Ashoka/State Emblem of India, with motto from the Mundaka Upanishad: Satyameva Jayate *[Truth alone Triumphs].*

The earliest Upanishads are the Great Forest and Chandogya [from *chanda*, poetic metre, prosody], which date from around or before the sixth century BCE. The Chandogya and Great Forest (or Brihadaranyaka), which are compiled from even older texts, are also the longest Upanishads, with, respectively, 627 and 434 verses; while the shortest *mukhya* Upanishads are the Mandukya and Isha, with only 12 and 18 verses.

The Mandukya discusses Om, Brahman, and four states of consciousness. The Isha (or Ishopanishad), is often given pride of place at the beginning of Upanishadic anthologies. In an abridged form, it runs something like this:

> Behold the universe in the glory of God: and all that lives and moves on earth. Leaving the transient, find joy in the Eternal ... He who sees all beings in his own Self, and his own Self in all beings loses all fear ... May life go to immortal life, and the body go to ashes, Om. O my soul, remember past strivings, remember! O my soul, remember past strivings, remember!

Although it is the philosophy and poetry that are retained, the content of the Upanishads is very diverse. The Upanishads fit into the Vedic tradition, and, like the Brahmanas and Aranyakas, may include mantras, rituals, creation myths, lineages of teachers, historical narratives, and the like. At their best and most original, they take the form of a philosophical dialogue, not unlike those of Plato, with named interlocutors presenting and debating various viewpoints. For example, in the Great Forest Upanishad, the sage Yajnavalkya engages in philosophical debate with, among others, his wife Maitreyi, the sage Gargi (another, rare, woman), and King Janaka of Videha —who salutes Yajnavalkya with 'namaste'. In the Chandogya Upanishad, the sage Uddalaka Aruni—the guru [teacher] of Yajnavalkya—engages in debate with his son, Shvetaketu. Uddalaka Aruni, Shvetaketu, Yajnavalkya, Maitreyi, and Gargi are among the first philosophers in recorded history.

This being philosophy, there is a tendency to abstraction, to grasp at 'the truth behind the truth' [*satyasya satyam*]. The central vision is one of pantheism (all is God) or panentheism (all is in God), with the Creator dissimulated in nature 'even as the silkworm is hidden in the web of silk he made'. God is

Brahman, and the part or aspect of Brahman that is in us is Atman. The aim then becomes to achieve the knowledge and unity of Atman and Brahman, which is wisdom, salvation, and liberation [*moksha*].

> As rivers flowing into the ocean find their final peace and their name and form disappear, even so the wise become free from name and form and enter into the radiance of the Supreme Spirit who is greater than all greatness. In truth who knows God becomes God.
>
> — MUNDAKA UPANISHAD

The student of Western philosophy might be reminded of Parmenides (d. c. 400 BCE), who, in his poem, *On Nature*, contrasted the Way of Truth to the Way of Opinion. Through a chain of strict *à priori* deductive arguments from premises deemed incontrovertible, Parmenides argued that, despite appearances (the Way of Opinion), the universe must consist of a single, undifferentiated, and indivisible unity, which he called 'the One'.

These verses from the Katha Upanishad could have been penned by Parmenides:

> Who sees the many and not the one, wanders on from death to death. Even by the mind this truth is to be learnt: there are not many but only one. Who sees variety and not the unity wanders on from death to death.

To bolster the philosophy of Parmenides, his student and lover Zeno of Elea produced a set of paradoxical arguments, including 'Achilles and the Tortoise', designed to undermine ordinary assumptions about motion, space, time, and plurality.

Just as Plato (d. 348 BCE) leaned upon Heraclitus and his Theory of Flux ('No one ever steps twice into the same river') for his conception of the sensible or phenomenal world, so he leaned upon Parmenides for his conception of the intelligible or noumenal world, which he rendered as the ideal, immutable realm of the Forms.

Plato's *Phaedo*, in which Socrates discusses the immortality of the soul with a pair of Pythagorean philosophers, is essentially an Upanishad, in both form and content. The philosopher, says Socrates (who is about to drink of the hemlock), aims at truth, but his body is constantly deceiving and distracting him:

> The body keeps us busy in a thousand ways because of its need for nurture... It fills us with needs, desires, fears, all sorts of illusions and much nonsense...

Absolute justice, absolute beauty, or absolute good cannot be apprehended by the senses, but only by pure thought, that is, by the mind or soul. Thus, the philosopher seeks in as far as possible to separate soul from body. As death is the complete separation of body and soul, the philosopher aims at death, and can be said to be almost dead.

This idea of the soul being waylaid by the body is also found in the Maitri Upanishad, which, remarkably, was written at around the same time as the *Phaedo*:

> The human soul rules the body; but the immortal spiritual soul is pure like a drop of water on a lotus leaf. The soul is under the power of the three constituents and conditions of nature [the three *gunas*] and thus it falls into confusion. Because of this confusion the soul cannot become conscious of the God who dwells within and whose power gives us power to work.

In Plato's *Phaedrus*, Socrates, having established its immortality, compares the soul to a chariot with a charioteer and two winged horses. Whereas the chariot of a god has two tame horses, that of a mortal has one tame horse and one unruly one which is the cause of much hardship for the charioteer.

This passage from the Katha Upanishad appears almost to be elucidating Plato's chariot allegory:

> Know the Atman as Lord of a chariot; and the body as the chariot itself. Know that reason is the charioteer; and the mind indeed is the reins. The horses, they say, are the senses; and their paths are the objects of sense. He who has not right understanding, and whose mind is never steady is not the ruler of his life, like a bad driver with wild horses.

Figure 9: Apollo's Chariot, by Odilon Redon (c. 1910). Stedelijk Museum, Amsterdam.

For more than two millennia, Western philosophers have been poring over Plato's elusive Form of the Good. Plato himself devised three interconnected allegories (the sun, line, and cave) merely to point at it. But I can tell you what it is in just one word: Brahman.

Plato even has a theory of reincarnation, leading us to suppose that he must, in a previous life, have been a Brahmana.

In 555 sutras, the *Brahma Sutra* (not to be confused with the Brahmanas) synthesizes and harmonizes the Upanishadic teachings on Brahman. The *Brahma Sutra*, also known as the *Vedanta Sutra*, is attributed to Badarayana, a sage of the first century BCE and the guru of Jaimini, who is credited with the *Mimamsa Sutra* of the Mimamsa darshana (Chapter 26). As the *Brahma Sutra* reviews and critiques other schools of thought, including Buddhism and Jainism, it must, at least in part, post-date the Buddha and Mahavira.

The *mukhya* Upanishads, the *Brahma Sutra*, and the *Bhagavad Gita* (collectively referred to as the *Prasthanatraya*, or 'Three Sources') became the basis of Vedanta (Chapter 26), which in turn became the dominant strand of Hindu philosophy. The sub-schools of Vedanta align according to the relation that they see between Atman and Brahman. The three main sub-schools are: Advaita (non-dualism, monism: Atman and Brahman are identical), Vishishtadvaita (qualified non-dualism: Atman and Brahman are similar but not identical), and Dvaita (dualism, theism: Atman and Brahman are distinct).

The Upanishads also exerted an important influence on the development of heterodox (non-Vedic) traditions such as Buddhism and Jainism (Chapters 9, 10, and 13).

Dara Shikoh (d. 1659 CE), the liberal heir apparent of the Mughal emperor Shah Jahan, translated fifty Upanishads into Persian so that they might be studied by Muslim scholars. In the introduction to the anthology, which he entitled *Sirr-i-Akbar* [*The Greatest Secret*], Dara suggests that the work referred to in the Qur'an as the *Kitab al-Maknun* [*Hidden Book*] is none other than the Upanishads. The Latin translation of the *Sirr-i-Akbar* by Anquetil-Duperron, published in 1802, had a tremendous impact on Schopenhauer. The Upanishads, he wrote, 'have been the solace of my life and will be the solace of my death' [Parerga 2, 185]. His *magnum opus*, *The World as Will...* (1818), leans heavily on Plato and the Upanishads.

Dara's defeat and execution by his brother Aurangzeb, who accused Dara of being influenced by Hinduism and abandoned the Mughal tradition of pluralism and religious tolerance, altered the course of history on the Indian subcontinent. But Dara, at least, had the consolation of eternity.

Some pearls from the Upanishads

> This earth is like honey for all beings, and all beings are like honey for this earth [the *madhu vidya*, or 'honey doctrine'].
>
> — GREAT FOREST UPANISHAD

> And in dreams the mind beholds its own immensity. What has been seen is seen again, and what has been heard is heard again. What has been felt in different places or faraway regions returns to the mind again. Seen and unseen, heard and unheard, felt and not felt, the mind sees all, since the mind is all.
>
> — PRASHNA UPANISHAD

Where there is creation there is progress. Where there is no creation, there is no progress: know the nature of creation.

Where there is joy there is creation. Where there is no joy there is no creation: know the nature of joy.

Where there is the Infinite there is joy. There is no joy in the finite. Only in the Infinite can there be joy: know the nature of the Infinite.

Where nothing else is seen, or heard, or known, there is the Infinite. Where something more is seen, or heard, or known, there is the finite. The finite is mortal; the Infinite, immortal.

— CHANDOGYA UPANISHAD

Awake, arise! Strive for the Highest, and be in the Light. Sages say the path is narrow and difficult to tread, narrow as the edge of a razor.

— KATHA UPANISHAD

Samsara, the transmigration of life, takes place in one's own mind. Let one therefore keep the mind pure, for what a man thinks that he becomes: this is a mystery of Eternity.

— MAITRI UPANISHAD

Those who in purity live in the solitude of the forest, who have wisdom and peace and long not for earthly possessions, those in radiant purity pass through the gates of the sun to the dwelling-place supreme where the Spirit is in Eternity.

— MUNDAKA UPANISHAD

6

BRAHMAN AND BRAHMA

It has been suggested that the root of 'Brahman' is *brh*, 'to grow or burst forth'. The word Brahman already appears in a number of Rig Vedic hymns, either in the neuter or the masculine. As a neuter noun, it denotes the voicing of the verses of the Vedas, which involves a release of breath and concomitant spiritual expansion and communion. This might explain the association of Brahman with Om—as when, in the Katha Upanishad, Yama tells Nachiketa that Om is 'the everlasting Brahman'. As a masculine noun, 'Brahman' refers to the priest who oversees the sacrifice.

Although Vedism is usually characterized as polytheistic, there is, from the very beginning, this idea that the various gods are manifestations of a single godhead:

> They call him Indra, Mitra, Varuna, Agni, and the celestial, great-winged Garutman; for although one, sages speak of Him diversely, calling him Agni, Yama, and Matarishvan.
>
> — RIG VEDA 1.164.46

The *Nasadiya Sukta* [Hymn of Creation, Rig Veda 10.129] refers to 'the One', adding that 'the gods came after, with the creation of the universe'. According to the *Nasadiya Sukta*, the gods do not know where this creation came from: only the One knows, 'or perhaps he does not.'

Rig Vedic proto-forms of Brahman (and Brahma) include Prajapati, the Lord of Creation, Purusha, the cosmic being, and Hiranyagarbha, the golden embryo or source of creation. According to the *Hiranyagarbha Sukta* [Rig Veda 10.121], 'Hiranyagarbha was present at the beginning; when born, he was the sole lord of created beings...' Prajapati's consort is said to be Vac, goddess of speech and mother of the Vedas.

In the Brahmana layer, the supreme creator is designated, for the first time, as Brahman—for example, in this verse from the Shatapatha Brahmana [10.2.3]: 'In the beginning this universe was just Brahman; Brahman created these gods.'

By the time of the Upanishads, Brahman had become the central concern, albeit as an abstract, impersonal principle. The Shvetashvatara Upanishad [1.16] describes Him as 'the Spirit Supreme', 'hidden in all things, as cream is hidden in milk.' The Kena Upanishad [1.3] describes him as 'the ear of the ear, the eye of the eye, and the Word of words, the mind of mind, and the life of life', before adding, 'We know not, we cannot understand, how he can be explained: He is above the known and he is above the unknown.' According to Yajnavalkya [Great Forest Upanishad 4.5.15, 3.8.8], Brahman can only be negatively described, as *neti, neti* ['neither this, nor that']: 'not coarse, not fine, not short, not long; without blood and without fat; without shadow and without darkness; without air and without space...' In other Upanishads, Brahman is variously described as Breath [Kaushitaki Upanishad 2.1], Wisdom [Aitareya Upanishad 3.3.7], the Self [Chandogya Upanishad 6.8.7], and Om.

Despite the difficulties and inconsistencies in defining him, Brahman is presented, in Aristotelian terms, as the prime or unmoved mover, the efficient, formal, and final cause of all that exists, and, at times, the material cause as well. Monotheism prevails as the other gods begin to bow down to Him: 'And the gods Agni, Vayu, and Indra excelled the other gods, for they were the first to reflect upon Brahman, and the first to recognize Him as the Spirit Supreme' [Kena Upanishad 4.2].

Brahman is sometimes referred to as Purusha, which, in the Upanishads, has come to refer to the eternal, unchanging universal principle, or consciousness. In some creation accounts, Brahman projects Himself into Purusha and Prakriti. Prakriti is material reality, or, more broadly, all that is subject to change, including our mind and psychology. Prakriti is made up of three *gunas* [qualities or tendencies of matter] known as *rajas* [creation, passion], *sattva* [preservation, harmony], and *tamas* [destruction, apathy], which, in combination, determine the character or nature of a person or thing.

In an oft quoted passage, the Maitri Upanishad [5.2] assimilates the *gunas* to what would later become the *Trimurti*, or Hindu Trinity, *rajas* to Brahma, *sattva* to Vishnu, and *tamas* to Rudra/Shiva: 'He being one, becomes three, becomes eight, becomes eleven, becomes twelve, becomes infinite.'

Purusha is closely associated with Atman, Prakriti with Maya. By learning to distinguish between the eternal and the ever-changing, we can bring ourselves to achieve the detachment that is liberation. The experience of realizing Brahman is described by Vedantins as *sat-chit-ananda* [truth-consciousness-bliss]. Although beyond thought and words, Brahman can be felt by each of us in the very core of our Being, Atman.

From the time of the Maitri Upanishad, Brahman becomes increasingly personified as the god Brahma. Within the Trimurti, Brahma represents the creative aspect of Brahman, with Vishnu representing the sustaining aspect and Shiva the destructive aspect. Both Shiva and Vishnu seek liberation from the creation of Brahman, the one by destroying it, the other by perfecting it.

In certain Puranas, such as the *Brahmananda Purana*, Brahma creates himself in the Hiranyagarbha, or golden egg, which emerges from an eternal ocean. When the egg hatches, he dreams the universe into existence. Among his *manasaputras* [mind-born sons] are the *saptarishi* [seven sages, cf. the Seven Sages of Greece], tasked with imparting the Vedas.

In a myth reminiscent of the Greek Pandora, related by Bhishma to Yudhishthira [*Mahabharata* 13.40], the gods, feeling threatened by the virtue of man, appeal to Brahma for help. In response, Brahma creates woman to delude mankind. 'For there is nothing more evil than women; a wanton woman is a blazing fire; she is the illusion born of Maya; she is the sharp edge of the razor; she is poison, a serpent, and death all in one.'

In Hindu iconography, Brahma is represented with four heads, facing in the four cardinal directions (Figure 10). The four heads represent, among others, the four Vedas, the four *yugas* [ages], the four *varnas* [castes], and the four *ashramas* [stages of life: student, householder, forest dweller, and renunciate]. Unusually for a Hindu god, his four arms carry no weapons but only symbols of knowledge and devotion such as a lotus and a rosary, and the four Vedas which he breathed out of his four mouths. He is seated on a lotus or on his *vahana* [mount], which is a *hamsa* [swan or goose]. His consort is Saraswati, goddess of learning, music, and the arts, who is one of the Tridevi with Lakshmi and Parvati.

Figure 10. Brahma on his hamsa. Pahari school, c. 1700.

By the seventh century CE, Brahma had lost his importance. Some sectarian texts portray him as a mere secondary creator, acting on behalf of Vishnu, Shiva, or Devi.

In the *Vishnu Purana*, he emerges out of a lotus blooming out of the navel of Vishnu in his recumbent Narayana form.

In the *Shiva Purana*, Vishnu and Brahma argue about who is the greater. As they debate, a pillar of light appears, and they decide to measure themselves by determining its source and extent. Vishnu adopts the form of the boar Varaha and journeys to the netherworld in search of its base; Brahma adopts the form of a gander and takes off into the heavens in search of its summit. When they are both returned, Vishnu concedes defeat, but Brahma claims to have overflown the pillar, and even recruits a ketaki flower to bear false witness and buttress his lie. Outraged by Brahma's deceit, Shiva emerges from the pillar of light in his fierce Bhairava form and cuts off one of Brahma's five heads. Shiva ordains that, henceforth, Brahma shall no longer receive worship.

Although there are in India only two temples dedicated to Brahma, a space is reserved for him, and Brahman, in every temple, in the central squares of the geometrical grid known as the *vastu-purusha-mandala*.

7

ATMAN, OR THE SELF

The story of the brahmin boy Nachiketa is retold in the Katha ['Distress'] Upanishad.

Vajashravasa purports to be sacrificing everything he owns, but his son Nachiketa notices that he is only bringing out those cows that are old, lame, or otherwise unproductive.

Nachiketa repeatedly taunts his father about this, saying, "I too am yours! To which god will you offer me?'" In a fit of rage, Vajashravasa cries out, "To Yama himself!"

Taking his father at his word, Nachiketa descends to Yama's deathly abode. But Yama is out, and the boy is made to wait for three days without food or water. When Yama returns, he offers the brahmin boy three boons to atone for his lack of hospitality.

For the first boon, Nachiketa asks for peace between himself and his father, when he is returned to the old man. Yama happily grants this. For the second boon, he asks to learn the fire sacrifice, which he performs to Yama's satisfaction. Finally, for the third boon, he asks to be told what comes after death...

Yama replies:

> Here, even the gods of yore had doubt. Indeed it is not easy to know—subtle is this matter—Oh, Nachiketa, ask for some other boon. Press not this on me; give this up for me ... ask for centenarian sons and grandsons, many cattle, elephants, gold and horses. Ask for wide extent of earth and live yourself, as many autumns as you like.

But Nachiketa is unswayed by the riches of the world, saying that man is not to be satisfied with wealth: 'If wealth were wanted, we shall get it, if we only see thee.'

Impressed, and flattered, by the boy, Yama agrees to tell him the Secret of the Self, which persists beyond the death of the body.

Many men choose the path of what is pleasant, but happiness comes only to those who choose the path of what is good:

> Living in the middle of ignorance and regarding themselves as intelligent and learned, the ignorant go round and round, in many crooked ways, like the blind led by the blind.

The knowledge of Atman cannot be reached by study, reason, or intelligence, but only by a pure, searching mind, such as that of Nachiketa...

After a time, Nachiketa bids farewell to Yama and returns to his father as a *jivanmukta*, one who has achieved *moksha* in this life.

What did Yama tell Nachiketa? And what, in the Chandogya Upanishad (Chapter 3), did Prajapati finally tell Indra, after having him wait for 101 years?

'Atman' [from *atma*, essence, breath] appears in the Rig Veda, albeit as a reflexive pronoun. Still, there is already the notion or intimation of a connection or correspondence between the individual self and the universal self, notably in the *Purusha Sukta*, in which the gods sacrifice a cosmic man to create the four *varnas* from its parts: the Brahmins from its mouth, the Kshatriyas from its arms, and so on.

In the Upanishads, Atman becomes the Self, although there are many conflicting definitions of Atman, which is variously described as Om, Brahman, the eternal self, the universal self, the sleeping self, breath, consciousness, fire-soul, mind, will... For instance, the Mandukya Upanishad [I.I] categorically states: 'All is Om. Brahman is all and Atman is Brahman.'

The relation of Atman to Brahman became the main bone of contention between the orthodox schools of Hindu philosophy. Some Upanishads, such as the Mandukya, claim or suggest that Atman and Brahman are the same; others, that Atman is only a part or aspect of Brahman. The synthesising *Brahma Sutr*a compromises between these positions: Atman is identical to Brahman, but only in the enlightened state.

Atman is normally translated into English as 'soul', but does not include the individual or cognitive aspects of the Judeo-Christian soul, and, for this reason, is better translated as 'Self'.

In Hindu thought, the individual aspects of the Judeo-Christian soul, such as ego, mind, reason, emotion, and desire, are subsumed under the *jivanatman* ['life-breath'], or *jiva* for short.

Whereas the jiva, the personal self, is enmeshed in *maya*, the Atman is detached from this particular life and incarnation. And whereas the jiva is ever-changing and evolving, the Atman, the universal Self, is steadfast and immoveable.

In the Shvetashvatara Upanishad [4.6], the jiva and Atman are compared to two inseparable birds sitting in a tree (the body). One bird, the jiva, gorges on the sweet and bitter fruits of the tree, while the other, tasting of neither, calmly looks on.

The Atman is neither the waking self, nor the dreaming self, nor the sleeping self, as Indra had been led to believe, but pure consciousness, or witness-consciousness, and of a kind with the supreme soul, *paramatman*, which is either Brahman or an aspect of Brahman.

In the Chandogya Upanishad, Uddalaka Aruni presents his son Shvetaketu with a series of analogies to cast light upon the nature of the self. In one such analogy [6.10], he tells Shvetaketu that, whereas some rivers run to the east, and others run to the west, they all end up losing themselves into the same ocean, from which they arose:

> That which is the subtlest of all is the Self of all this. It is the Truth. It is the Self. That thou art, O Shvetaketu.

This ultimate utterance, 'that thou art' [*tat tvam asi*], is perhaps better translated as, 'You too are like that, O Shvetaketu.'

Speaking of rivers, in his *Enneads* [5.1.2], Plotinus (d. 270 CE), the founder of Neo-Platonism, arrived, by a different course, to the very same vision:

> By the power of the soul the manifold and diverse heavenly system is a unit: through soul this universe is a God... This, by which the gods are divine, must be the oldest God of them all: and our own soul is of that same Ideal nature... If, then, it is the presence of soul that brings worth, how can a man slight himself and run after other things?

In all living things, Atman is the spark of life, or light of consciousness, that ignites and illumines all else for the time that it remains embodied. It is the eternal core of a living being, which, in death, leaves it for another form, or, at long last, returns to the infinity of Brahman.

Thus, although the Atman is detached, it must on some level be affected by the jiva, or long series of jivas, that it comes to be paired with. The first Jiva who recognizes it, on the back of all the jivas that went before, liberates it, and, by the same token, liberates itself. In a *jivanmukti* such as Nachiketa, the jiva and the Atman become as one.

Probably the most important point of difference between Hinduism and Buddhism (Chapter 10) is the Buddhist denial of Atman or any such eternal core.

If the Self, the Atman, is made out of the same stuff as the world, then self-understanding and self-control become means of understanding and controlling the world, and existing on a higher plane. In the Kathopanishad [1.2.20], Yama tells Nachiketa: 'Subtler than the subtle, greater than the great, in the heart of each living being, the Atman reposes. One free from desire, with his mind and the senses composed, sees the glory of the Atman and becomes absolved from grief.' In the Chandogya Upanishad [8.7.1], Prajapati declares: 'There is a Spirit which is pure and which is beyond old age and death; and beyond hunger and thirst and sorrow. This is Atman, the Spirit in man. All the desires of this Spirit are Truth. It is this Spirit that we must find and know: man must find his own Soul. He who has found and knows his Soul has found all the worlds, has achieved all his desires.' It is this decree that set Indra and Virochana on their quest to find the Secret of the Self.

> It is not speech which we should want to know, but the speaker. It is not things seen which we should want to know, but the seer. It is not sounds which we should want to know, but the hearer. It is not mind which we should want to know, but the thinker.
>
> — KAUSHITAKI UPANISHAD 3.8

Knowledge of the self can be attained through the practice of yoga, which Yama defines for Nachiketa as 'the firm holding back of the senses' [Kathopanishad 2.3.10-11]: 'When the five organs of perception become still, together with the mind, and the intellect ceases to be active: that is called the highest state.' This is the first ever mention of 'yoga' in its modern sense, and it is by Death himself! Yama warns Nachiketa to be watchful, 'for Yoga comes and goes.'

> Contemplating with a concentrated mind, weaned from all external objects on the Atman, ancient, hard to see, lodged in the inmost recess, located in intelligence, and seated amongst miserable surroundings, the man of intelligence renounces joy and grief.
>
> — KATHA UPANISHAD 1.2.12

Even with yoga, knowledge of the Self is no easy thing. Atman-Brahman may be so fundamental that it cannot be understood, even by the few.

In another of his analogies [Chandogya Upanishad 6.12], Uddalaka asks Shvetaketu to fetch the fruit of a banyan and cut it open. "What do you see?" asks Uddalaka. "These tiny seeds" says Shvetaketu. "Now break one of them open. What do you see there?" "Nothing, Father."

> O Somya [worthy of, or inspired by, soma], the finest part in that seed is not visible to you. But in that finest part lies hidden the huge banyan tree. Have faith in what I say, O Somya. That which is the subtlest of all is the Self of all this. It is the Truth. It is the Self. That thou art [You too are like that], O Shvetaketu.

Another difficulty is that the Self is too close to be seen, located as it is behind the eyes—behind, even, the mind. In the Great Forest Upanishad [4.5.15], Yajnavalkya asks his wife Maitreyi: 'By what means can one perceive the perceiver?'

As the banyan fruit experiment suggests, the Self is not some core or centre, how ever minuscule, but pervades all of consciousness. In that sense, the self that Indra had determined to find never existed.

In a third analogy, Uddalaka asks Shvetaketu to dissolve a lump of salt into some water, and then bids him to fetch the salt. But, of course, the boy cannot find the salt, even though it pervades the water—and will remain long after it has evaporated. For now, all he can do is taste, or experience, the salt.

The pan-Indian traditions of non-violence and vegetarianism, and kindness and tolerance, are rooted in the Atman-Brahman doctrine, which implies a commonality, or shared divinity, between all living creatures.

The connection is already made in the Chandogya Upanishad [8.15.1], which in its parting words recommends that a man who has finished his studies 'keeps all his senses under control and avoids violence unless he is at a holy place.'

> This is how he lives his whole life. Then after death he goes to Brahmaloka, and he is not born again, he is not born again.

8

KARMA, SAMSARA, MOKSHA, YOGA

In early Vedic texts, *karma* [from *karman*, action, deed] referred only to ritual and sacrificial actions. However, the Rig Veda already contains the concept of cosmic law and order, in the form of *rita*, which is upheld by Varuna. Over time, *rita* evolved into *dharma* ['duty'] and *karma*.

The earliest recognizable theories of *karma* and *samsara* [rebirth] are in the Upanishads, and may have been inspired by the indigenous, non-Aryan *shramana* [striver] tradition of wandering ascetics. The *shramana* movement would later give rise to Buddhism and Jainism.

In the Great Forest Upanishad [3.2.13], Yajnavalkya says that 'a man becomes good by good work and bad by bad work'.

Later [4.4.5], he elaborates on this point:

> Now as a man is like this or like that, according as he acts and according as he behaves, so will he be: a man of good acts will become good, a man of bad acts, bad. He becomes pure by pure deeds, bad by bad deeds. And here they say that a person

> consists of desires, and as is his desire, so is his will; and as is his will, so is his deed; and whatever deed he does, that he will reap.

This, I think, is the earliest formulation of the famous epigram variously attributed to the Buddha, Lao Tzu, Ralph Waldo Emerson, and others: 'Watch your thoughts. They become words. Watch your words. They become deeds. Watch your deeds. They become habits. Watch your habits. They become character. Character is everything.'

At this stage, Yajnavalkya is tying actions to character, rather than to reward and punishment in this or another life. His words would not be out of place in the *Nicomachean Ethics*, in which Aristotle (d. 322 BCE) argues that, in the main, moral virtues are acquired by custom and habit.

Further on in the Great Forest Upanishad [6.2], Shvetaketu, thinking to have completed his education, travels to the court of King Pravahana of Panchala. To test his knowledge, Pravahana asks him five questions, including where people go after death. Unable to answer any of the questions, Shvetaketu returns to his father Uddalaka Aruni and faults him for his teaching. Uddalaka says that he would have taught him the answers to the questions, had he known them. So father and son go to Pravahana, who agrees to take them in as students—an unusual case of Brahmanas learning from a Kshatriya. Pravahana teaches them the so-called doctrine of the five fires and two paths in the afterlife, which explains human and natural life cycles in highly allegorical, ritual-sacrificial terms.

This story is repeated in the Chandogya Upanishad [5.3] with minor variations and a verse [5.10.7], suspected of being a later addition, that is missing from the Great Forest Upanishad:

> Now, people of good conduct attain a good birth accordingly, like that of a Brahmin, Kshatriya, or Vaishya, whereas people of bad conduct attain a bad birth, like that of a dog, pig, or casteless person.

In any case, by the time of the *Mahabharata* (circa fourth century BCE), the doctrines of karma and samsara are fully formed, and there has been a definite shift from the ritualism of the Vedas and five fires towards philosophy, asceticism, and mysticism. The *Laws of Manu* (circa first century CE) are premised on the doctrine of karma and samsara, which is laid out in that work's final chapter (Chapter 16).

Karma, often misunderstood as fate or destiny, is the causal law by which our modes of engagement come to determine our station and situation. It is the law of cause and effect extended to human affairs, so that every instance of thought, speech, and action is a cause, and all our experiences are their effects. Good and bad karma are often referred to as *punya* ['merit'] and *paap* ['demerit']. Even if *punya* does not immediately pay off, or seem to pay off, it does in the long run, which is why karma is tied to samsara, with future births conditioned by the accumulated balance of paap and punya.

At the outset of Plato's *Republic*, the sophist Thrasymachus argues that it is not the just but the unjust who flourish, and that the tyrant, being the most unjust of people, is also the happiest. At the end of the *Republic*, in the Myth of Er, Plato resorts to reincarnation to guarantee that the genuinely just always come out on top, with each soul choosing its next life according to its wisdom. In this and other things, Plato was influenced by Pythagoras (d. 495 BCE), who, like the Indians, came to believe in the transmigration of the soul.

Although karma is individual, it can in certain circumstances be transferred, for example, from a dying father to his son—the son being, essentially, the continuation of the father. This rite, in which the father places himself above his son, and touches his organs with his own, is laid out in the Kaushitaki Upanishad [2.15]. More ordinarily, the *paap* of a person, living or deceased, may be mitigated by the prayers and pilgrimages of others.

As discussed, karma serves the same purpose as Eden in providing the major motivation to lead a moral life. In the Christian tradition, the soul of the newly deceased is judged and sent to heaven, hell, or purgatory. Then, there is also a Last Judgement that takes place after the Second Coming of Christ and the resurrection of the dead. In the Letter to the Galatians [6.7], St Paul warns: 'Be not deceived; God is not mocked: for whatsoever a man soweth, that shall he also reap.'

According to the Old Testament, punishment might even be extended to later generations, that is, to future selves:

> The LORD is long-suffering, and of great mercy, forgiving iniquity and transgression, and by no means clearing the guilty, visiting the iniquity of the fathers upon the children unto the third and fourth generation.
>
> — NUMBERS 14:18 (KJV)

Karma also serves other purposes, such as accounting for the existence of evil, rationalizing rebirth (which could also operate independently of karma), and providing a soteriological goal of final liberation. In determining our circumstances and even our temperament, karma may constrict our options, but it does not deprive us of choice and deliberation, enabling it to condone social inequities and the caste system (Chapter 16) while at the same time affirming human freedom.

The importance of karma, and the degree of freedom and determination within it, is a point of difference between the Hindu schools. But even if karma theory is not literally true, it is at least metaphorically true. Being good does generally pay off, if only in peace of mind and mental health. In which case, is karma theory a firm basis for morality, or merely an appeal to self-interest? One way around this problem, which has been taken, is to broaden the scope of karma to include thoughts as well as actions, so that the system becomes impossible to game.

Doing the right thing for the wrong reason is not the same, and does not feel the same, as doing it for the right reason. Having expounded on karma theory [Great Forest Upanishad 4.4.5, quoted above], Yajnavalkya explains that those who are attached to their deeds return to 'this world of action', whereas those who are free from desires, or desire only the Self, being Brahman, go to Brahman. The truly virtuous act is the one that is desireless. Like the Stoic archer, one must concentrate on doing the right thing, to the best of one's ability, without at all being attached to the outcome. For it is from attachment that life and misery arise.

The Buddha had another way around the problem, which is to deny the metaphysical distinction between self and others, so that helping others is tantamount to helping oneself. Aristotle makes a similar move in the *Nicomachean Ethics*, when he says that there is no conflict between helping a friend and helping oneself insofar as a perfect friend is like another self. When we are good to another, we are good to all, including ourself, because the distinction is an illusion, and karma travels.

If we have no self, why did the Buddhists not altogether give up on karma and samsara? In part, because karma can still operate in the absence of an Atma, with future incarnations being conditioned by the sum of all the karmic actions that have been put into the world. Every person, their parents, their teachers, and their parents and their teachers, is the embodiment of every karmic action that has ever gone before. Our every action reverberates to the end of time.

Although rebirth, especially the slightly better rebirth that most people hope for, sounds better than death, the ultimate goal is to escape rebirth. In a sense, the ultimate goal is a proper death, or return to Brahman. This release from samsara, called *(vi)moksha* [from *muc*, 'to free'] or *(vi)mukti*, is realized through self-knowledge. The conversation with Yama in the Katha Upanishad (Chapter 7) is among the earliest expositions of samsara and moksha. Enlightened by their exchange, Nachiketa leaves as a *jivanmukta*, one who has achieved moksha in this life—as opposed to after death, a *videhamukta*.

Until the Upanishads, the Vedas repeatedly refer to the three aims of human life, or *purusharthas*: *dharma*, *artha* [prosperity], and *kama* [pleasure]. All three are important, but, of course, in cases of conflict, duty must prevail over artha and kama. Later, a fourth purushartha, moksha, is added to the *trivarga* of dharma, artha, and kama.

Although moksha becomes the ultimate goal of human life, it is, in fact, in conflict with dharma, since one cannot be both a householder and a renunciate. By assimilating the four purusharthas with the four *ashramas* [stages of life: student, householder, forest dweller, and renunciate], it becomes possible to envisage each purushartha as a separate stage of life. Alternatively, or in addition, it might be rationalized that being a good householder, or a good warrior, or a good king, is itself a form of renunciation, and not only because renunciates depend on the services of others. The tensions between the purusharthas reflect the tensions within the Vedas.

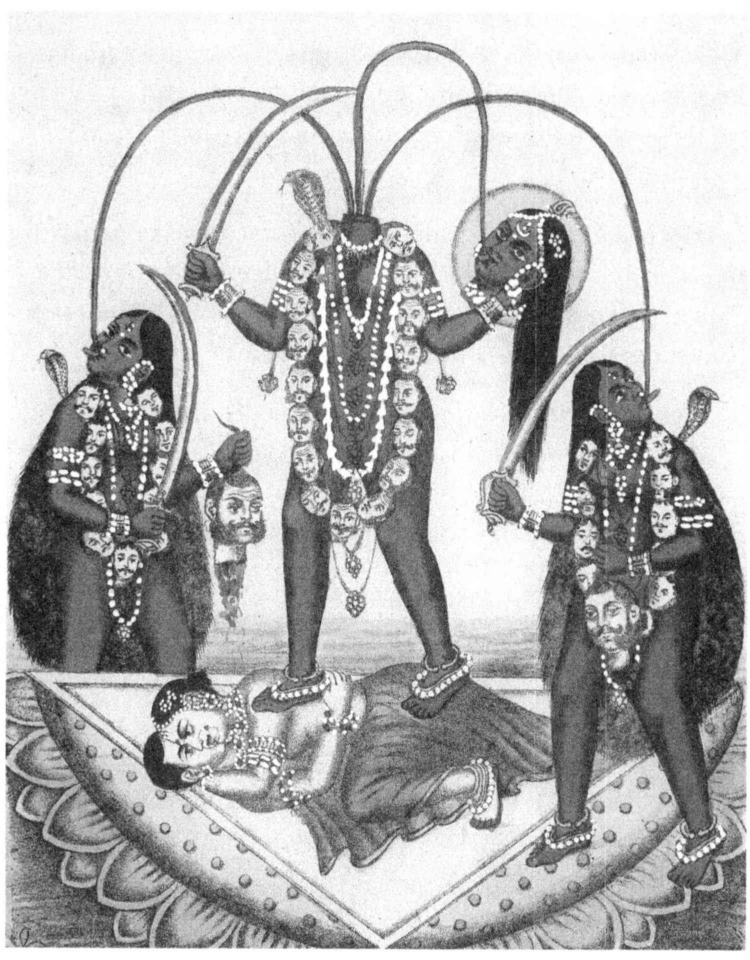

Figure 11. The tantric goddess Chhinnamasta. Trampling upon Kama and his wife Rati, she severs her own head to separate Self from body and create life from death.

Moksha, as has been said, comes from self-knowledge (that is, knowledge of Atman-Brahman), which, as indicated by Yama, can be attained through the practice of yoga [from *yuj*, 'to join', 'to yoke', 'to unite'].

In the *Bhagavad Gita*, Krishna outlines three yogas or paths to moksha: Jnana Yoga, the Path of Knowledge; Karma Yoga, the Path of (selfless) Action; and Bhakti Yoga, the Path of Devotion (surrender to God, as epitomized by the Hare Krishnas).

To these, a fourth yoga is sometimes added, Raja Yoga, the Path of Meditation—which, in around the eleventh century CE, came to include Hatha Yoga (the physical sort of yoga familiar to Westerners) as preparation for meditation.

I shall return to yoga in Chapters 21 and 24.

9

LIFE OF THE BUDDHA

The Buddha's dates are uncertain, and range from 624 BCE (earliest birth) to 368 BCE (latest death).

According to Buddhist scriptures, the Buddha, or Siddhartha Gautama, had a friend—and, later, a disciple—in King Bimbisara of Magadha, placing him firmly in the period of the Mahajanapadas (sixth to fourth centuries BCE), also known, after the decline of the Indus Valley Civilization, as the second urbanization period.

Whatever his dates, the Buddha began as a wandering ascetic, or *shramana* [striver], and lived for some 80 years. Setting aside Harappan artefacts such as the Pashupati seal (Figure 3), which depicts a cross-legged figure, the earliest evidence of a yogic tradition in India is found in the Rig Vedic Keshin Hymn:

> The Munis, girdled with the wind, wear garments soiled of yellow hue. They, following the wind's swift course, go where the Gods have gone before.
>
> — RIG VEDA 10.136.2

The Buddha's movement, Buddhism, arose in reaction to the increasing remoteness and abstruseness of Vedic Brahmanism. The Brahmanas regarded the Buddhists as *nastika*, that is, non-believers in the Vedas, and, by extension, non-believers in God —laying the ground for the theism of later Hinduism.

Today, Buddhism is the most studied of the heterodox *nastika* schools of Indian philosophy, followed by Jainism, Charvaka, Ajivika, and Ajnana. The chief orthodox, or *astika*, schools, which accept the authority of the Vedas (or, at least, do not explicitly reject it) are Samkhya, Yoga, Nyaya, Vaisheshika, Mimamsa, and Vedanta (Chapters 24-26).

His followers deified the Buddha, and, accordingly, mythologized his life; and it would be profitless to try, if that were possible, to separate the mythology from the reality.

According to tradition, then, the Buddha was born in Lumbini, in what is now southern Nepal, to King Shuddhodana of the Shakya clan. The Shakyas lived in an oligarchic republic, so Shuddhodana, though a leader, may have been something less than a king. Siddhartha was raised in the Shakya capital, Kapilavastu, and would spend most of his life in what is now Bihar and Uttar Pradesh, on the eastern margins of Aryavarta and Vedic Brahmanism.

Shuddhodana's wife, Mahamaya, dreamt of a white elephant with six tusks entering her right side. Ten lunar months later, while strolling in a garden in Lumbini, she grabbed onto the drooping branch of a sal tree, and Siddhartha ['He who has achieved his aim'] emerged fully formed from under her right arm. Siddhartha proceeded to take seven steps, before declaring that this would be his last life.

Seven days later, Mahamaya died. The court astrologers predicted that Siddhartha would become either a *chakravartin* [universal monarch] or a *buddha* [enlightened one]. Not wishing to lose his son and heir—and, at that, a future chakravartin—to a life of renunciation, Shuddhodana confined him to a life of luxury within the precinct of the palace, where he would not be exposed to religious teaching or human suffering. At the age of 16, Siddhartha married the beautiful princess Yashodhara, and everything seemed on track for Shuddhodana.

But at the age of 29, having tired of the delights of the royal kitchen and harem, Siddhartha asked to make a chariot ride through the city. The king agreed, but had all the old, infirm, and otherwise poor cleared from the route. Even so, Siddhartha did, for the very first time, catch a glimpse of an old man. He asked Channa, his charioteer: "Am I also subject to this?"

With his curiosity piqued, Siddhartha made three more sorties outside the palace gates, seeing, in turn, a diseased man, a decaying corpse, and, finally, a meditating mendicant, whose serene smile inspired him to join the path in search of freedom from suffering.

Siddhartha renounced his position, wealth, and family to take up the life of a wandering ascetic. As night fell and he prepared to make his escape, he was told that a son had been born to him. He went into Yashodara's chamber to look upon his sleeping wife and son, and named the boy Rahula [Fetter, on the path to enlightenment]. Having crossed the Anoma River into the forest, he sent back the faithful Channa along with his weapons, jewels, and hair. He even sent back his beloved horse, Kanthaka, who died from a broken heart.

In the *Genealogy of Morality*, Nietzsche seizes upon Siddhartha's desertion of his family to support his argument that 'a married philosopher belongs in a comedy':

> Every philosopher would speak as once Buddha spoke when someone told him of the birth of his son, "Rahula has been born to me. A shackle has been forged for me." ... *Perat mundus, fiat philosophia, fiat philosophus, fiam!* [Let the world perish, but not philosophy, not the philosopher, not me!]
>
> — ON THE GENEALOGY OF MORALITY 3.7

In the forest, Siddhartha adopted the life of a mendicant, or beggar. For the next six years, he practised successively under two teachers of meditation. With five friends, he subjected himself to extreme forms of self-mortification, gradually reducing his daily meal to a single grain of rice.

One day, he accepted a bowl of *kheera* [milk-rice pudding] from a farmer's wife called Sujata, who had mistaken the skeletal waif for a wish-granting tree spirit (Figure 12). With some food in the belly, he concluded that extreme asceticism would not advance him along the path to freedom from suffering, but serve only to cloud his mind.

On the full moon of May, six years after having left the palace, the 35-year-old Siddhartha sat in meditation under a peepul tree. The demon Mara tried to disrupt him, including by sending his daughters to seduce him.

When Mara challenged his right to occupy the ground on which he sat, he touched the earth with his right hand, and the goddess of the earth confirmed with a tremor that he had earned this right—on account of a great gift which he had made in his previous life as Prince Vessantara.

Through the night, he had visions of his past lives. Then at dawn he reached enlightenment and became a Buddha.

Figure 12. Sandstone head of the fasting Buddha, whom Sujata mistook for a wish-granting tree spirit. Gandhara, second or third century CE. British Museum, London. The Greco-Buddhist Gandhara school produced the first representations of the Buddha in human form, ending the early period of aniconism in Buddhism.

The peepul tree, *Ficus religiosa*, is now better known as the bodhi tree, and the place where the Buddha sat in meditation as Bodh Gaya ['Place of Enlightenment']. Representations of the Buddha often include his earth-touching gesture, known as the *bhumisparsha mudra*.

The Buddha remained in the vicinity of the bodhi tree to savour his enlightenment. When a seven-day storm blew up, the serpent king Mucalinda encircled him seven times with his coils and sheltered him with his seven-headed hood (Figure 13).

After seven weeks, the Buddha got up to teach. He delivered his first sermon in the deer park at Sarnath, on the outskirts of Kashi [modern-day Varanasi], preaching the Middle Way between luxury and austerity, as well as the Four Noble Truths and Eightfold Path (Chapter 10). In his second sermon, he presented his doctrine of *anatman* [no-self]. So eloquently did he speak that, upon hearing him, his five ascetic friends rose up into *arhats* [those who have gained such insight as to escape samsara/achieve Nirvana]. They became the first members of the Buddhist monastic order known as the *sangha*.

For the next 45 years, the Buddha spread his teachings across northeast India, followed by wandering ascetics and laypersons who supported the ascetics. Although many of his followers imitated him in renouncing the life of the householder, most were not so ambitious. Over the years, many of the renouncers settled into monasteries funded by prominent members of the laity. The Buddha delivered many of his discourses in the monastery of Jetavana in Shravasti, the capital of Kosala, which had been donated to him by the banker Anathapindada. Monks severed ordinary ties to family and community to become 'islands unto themselves'. They could eat meat if it was offered to them, but only after ensuring that the animal had not been slaughtered on their behalf.

Figure 13. Naga-enthroned Buddha, Angkor, twelfth century CE. Cleveland Museum of Art.

When Mahamaya's sister Mahapajapati, who had been his foster-mother and become his step-mother, asked to be ordained, the Buddha refused her, owing, perhaps, to fears around the safety of nuns. But when pressed, he relented, and Mahapajapati became the first *bhikkhuni* [Buddhist nun]. A benefit of becoming a bhikkhuni was to escape a woman's restricted dharma, which was to be a devoted wife and mother. In time, Yashodhara too became a bhikkhuni. When Rahula asked for his patrimony, his father ordained him a monk.

However, the Buddha refused to appoint his radically austere cousin Devadatta as his successor. Bitterly aggrieved, Devadatta tried three times to kill him, by means of assassins, a boulder, and an elephant, which arrested its charge to bow at his feet. The schism was repaired when the earth sucked Devadatta down into Naraka, or Hell.

In Kushinagara, the Buddha, now around 80 years old, succumbed to a tainted piece of either mushroom or pork. His chief disciple, Mahakashyapa, ignited the funeral pyre, after which his relics were distributed and enshrined in large mound-like structures called stupas.

According to Buddhist tradition, in the third century BCE, the Mauryan emperor Ashoka (Chapter 14) gathered the relics from seven of the eight stupas and erected 84,000 stupas to distribute them across India. Some of Ashoka's stupas, such as the Great Stupa at Sanchi and the Dhamek Stupa at Sarnath, remain important pilgrimage sites.

10

BUDDHIST PHILOSOPHY

The Buddha was struck by human suffering, and spent years trying to understand its causes and the means to overcome them.

Two early insights that led him to enlightenment are the Middle Way and Dependent Origination. According to the doctrine of the Middle Way, we are more likely to achieve insight and wisdom if we avoid extremes of self-gratification and self-mortification. According to the doctrine of Dependent Origination, or Interdependent Arising, life is a continuous process of change, and every instance of change has manifold causes and effects. This means that all things are conditioned by other things, so that all things are interconnected. Suffering arises from a craving for permanence; but all permanence is an illusion that, in time, can only lead to pain and disappointment. Although nothing exists permanently, it is equally wrong to say that nothing exists at all. This, too, is a middle way. Does the self exist? In a sense it does; in another sense, it does not—which is why, when asked the question, the Buddha, as was his way, simply remained silent.

The Middle Way and Dependent Origination pervade all aspects of Buddhist philosophy. After the Buddha, the most noted Buddhist philosopher is Nagarjuna (d. c. 250 CE), who founded or re-founded the Madhyamaka ['Middle Way'] school, an important strand of Mahayana (Great Vehicle) Buddhism. In the *Mulamadhyamakakarika* [*Root Verses on the Middle Way*], Nagarjuna argues that between the extremes of permanence and nothingness lies emptiness, or *shunyata*. Although they exist, all phenomena are 'empty' insofar as they lack permanence or autonomous existence.

Although this sounds pessimistic—and Nagarjuna has been accused of being a nihilist—it is precisely this emptiness and fluidity that underlies the possibility of change and creation. In Zen Buddhism, a more dynamic alternative to the *koan*, or riddle, is for the master to suddenly slap his student to shake him out of who he thinks he is and what he thinks he's doing.

In his *Dispeller of Disputes*, Nagarjuna responds to critics who accused his theory of emptiness of itself being empty by protesting that he must, of necessity, work within conventions of thought and language: if there is silence, to call it out would be to break the silence, though this need not mean that there is, or was, no silence.

If all things are conditional, and subject to change, then so too is suffering. It is said that, upon enlightenment, the Buddha understood the Four Noble Truths—more accurately translated as the 'four truths for the noble of spirit'—which he outlined in his first sermon:

1. Suffering [*dukkha*] is inherent in all life.
2. The cause of all suffering is desire.
3. There is a natural way to eliminate all suffering.
4. The Noble Eightfold Path is that way.

The first truth, *dukkha*, acknowledges the unsatisfactory nature of existence. The second truth, *samudaya* [origin], attributes a cause to this suffering. The third truth, *nirodha* [cessation], posits a state, comparable to the Greek *ataraxia* [tranquillity], that is free from suffering. And the fourth truth, *marga* [path], points to the method for achieving that state.

Although translated as 'suffering', *dukkha* refers more broadly to the inherently impermanent and unsatisfactory nature of all things, including the pleasant ones—for, really, it is on account of them that we suffer most. *Nirodha* is also referred to as *nibbana* ['blown out', 'extinguished', as in a candle] in Pali or *nirvana* in Sanskrit, indicating that, rather than a positive state, nirvana is more of a negative state of absence of desire. Nirvana is the state of wishing for nothing, not even nirvana.

If the cause of dukkha is desire, the cause of desire is ignorance, pointing to knowledge or wisdom as the way forward. With proper perspective, there would be no desire, and so no suffering—and no (re)birth, which is the outcome of desire, and the source of all suffering. Does this mean that people ought to refrain from having children? No, insofar as being born is an opportunity to escape being born. The purpose of life is to provide us with an opportunity to escape it, by achieving wisdom. Otherwise, we shall have to try again.

Unfortunately, wisdom is hard to attain, because it runs counter to everything we have learnt and everything we love, including the thing we love most, our self. On top of that, it skirts with everything we fear, not least death and impermanence. For these reasons and more, it takes long practice and training to attain wisdom, and even longer practice and training to hold on to it in the face of temptation, fragility, and adversity.

But even if we are unable to commit to becoming a monk or nun, we can still embark on the Noble Eightfold Path:

1. Right view (maintaining perspective on reality)
2. Right intention or resolve (renouncing the worldly life for the life of wisdom)
3. Right speech (e.g. no lies, slanders, or idle talk)
4. Right action or conduct (e.g. no killing, stealing, or sexual misconduct)
5. Right livelihood (earning a living through a profession that does not visit harm on others)
6. Right effort (preventing unwholesome mental states, and encouraging wholesome, productive ones)
7. Right mindfulness (paying due attention to thoughts, feelings, sensations, and external phenomena)
8. Right concentration or meditation (cultivating the highest states of mind)

The eight categories are overlapping and mutually reinforcing, and to be worked on simultaneously rather than successively. Indeed, the Noble Eightfold Path is often represented by a dharma wheel, or *dharmachakra*, with eight spokes, none of which is either first or last (Figure 14). The wheel of dharma can also stand for dependent origination, change, and samsara, all in one. It is said that, with his first sermon, the Buddha set the wheel of dharma into motion.

With desire under firm control, everything becomes a lot better, and a lot easier. In an absence of desire, why lie or steal, or be envious or greedy? Or why be anxious, or angry, or depressed? The opposite of envy is not merely an absence of envy, but shared joy and admiration. The opposite of greed is not merely an absence of greed, but decency and generosity. The opposite of anger is not merely an absence of anger, but compassion. The opposite of anxiety is not merely an absence of anxiety, but tranquillity. The opposite of depression is not merely an absence of depression, but wisdom.

Figure 14. Wheel of the chariot of the sun, Konark Sun Temple, Odisha. 1250 CE. The temple is designed as a chariot with 24 such wheels. As a symbol, the wheel of dharma has been adopted by several Indian religions, including Hinduism, Buddhism, and Jainism. The 24-spoke Ashoka dharmachakra features on the flag of India.

How is it that the self can both exist and not exist? The self, or 'not-self' [*anatta*], is composed of five elements [*skandhas*], namely, body, sensation, perception, will, and consciousness. The five skandhas are in a constant state of flux but together create for the not-self the illusion of integrity and continuity, that is, the illusion of the self.

This explains why, when I try to become aware of myself, I can only ever become aware of such and such perception, such and such sensation, or such and such thought, but never of any actual, core self.

Try it now for yourself...

The death of the bodily self leads to the disaggregation of the skandhas and to their re-aggregation into another not-self which is neither identical to nor entirely different from the previous one, but that forms part of a causal continuum with it.

An analogy that is often offered to describe this process of rebirth is that of a flame, fuelled by desire, passing from one candle to the next.

The cycle of rebirth can only be broken if the self is able to transcend its subjective and distorted image of the world, which is built around the 'I am' conceit. This, then, is nibbana, or nirvana. Nirvana, as I see it, rests on the understanding that consciousness is a sequence of conscious moments rather than the continuous, unbroken consciousness of the 'I am' conceit.

If this all sounds rather mystical, consider that the empiricist philosopher David Hume (d. 1776) independently arrived at a similar view:

> For my part, when I enter most intimately into what I call myself, I always stumble on some particular perception or other, of heat or cold, light or shade, love or hatred, pain or pleasure. I can never catch myself at any time without a perception, [or] observe anything but the perception. When my perceptions are removed for a time, as by sound sleep, so long am I insensible to myself, and may truly be said not to exist. And were all my perceptions removed by death, and could I neither think, nor feel, nor see, nor love... after the dissolution of my body, I should be entirely annihilated... [Anyone with a different notion of himself] may, perhaps, perceive something simple and continued ... although I am certain there is no such principle in me.
>
> — A TREATISE OF HUMAN NATURE, 1.4.6

Our ego defences as broadly conceived—that is, not only our ego defences proper but also our habits, customs, culture, and other ties—may provide us with an illusion of self, but they also define us as such and such, and, in so doing, constrain our range of thought, feeling, and action. Paradoxically, the very elements that furnish us with our sense of self are also those that prevent us from fulfilling our true promise and potential as human beings.

As I argue in my book on the psychology of self-deception, it is only by renouncing the self, that is, by dropping her defences and committing symbolic suicide, that a person is able to open up to different modes of being and relating and transform herself into a pure essence of humanity. In so doing, she becomes free to recast herself as a more joyful and productive person, and attains the only species of transcendence and immortality that is open to us, mere mortals.

And so, if we are to live, we must first learn to die.

After the death of the Buddha, Buddhism remained a small sect for several centuries before being championed by the Mauryan emperor Ashoka (Chapter 14).

The first major schism occurred in the aftermath of the Second Buddhist Council, which took place about a hundred years after the death of the Buddha. After that, there were several more schisms, and many schools came and went.

Founded in 427 under the Guptas (Chapter 23), the *mahavihara* [monastic university] of Nalanda, in Magadha, played an important part in the development of Mahayana and Vajrayana Buddhism. Regarded as the world's first residential university, it is being revived, in name at least, by the Indian government.

Nalanda fell into abeyance in 1197 CE, by which time Buddhism had almost vanished from India, with the Buddha successfully integrated into Hinduism as the ninth avatar of Vishnu. Even today, following a revival of sorts led by the Dalit BR Ambedkar (Chapter 16), there are more Buddhists in Cambodia or even Taiwan than there are in India. In India, there are fewer than 10 million Buddhists, compared to around 250 million in China and 500 million worldwide.

The three most important extant schools are Theravada (the School of the Elders), Mahayana (The Great Vehicle), and Vajrayana (The Way of the Diamond), sometimes referred to as, respectively, South Asian Buddhism, East Asian Buddhism, and Northern or Tibetan or Tantric Buddhism. Vajrayana, headed by the Dalai Lama, might be considered an offshoot of Mahayana, as might Zen.

Theravada, sometimes condescendingly referred to as Hinayana ['Lesser Vehicle'] by Mahayana Buddhists, claims to be the oldest and most orthodox school. Naturally, the reformist Mahayana movement disputes the Theravada claim of being closer to the Buddha's original teachings.

The most important point of difference between the two schools is that the end of Theravada is individual liberation, whereas the end of Mahayana is liberation with a view to the liberation of others—meaning that an enlightened Mahayana Buddhist may choose, out of compassion, to remain for a time in the cycle of samsara.

If you are one such *bodhisattva* hanging around in samsara, please send me an email.

11

THE JATAKA TALES

The Three Jewels [Triratna] to which Buddhists go for refuge are the: Buddha, Dharma [doctrine, teaching], and Sangha [monastic order, community]. The imperishable Dharma [Pali: *Dhamma*] is regarded as a raft for crossing over, not merely clinging onto like modern self-help.

The Pali Canon of the Theravada school is the most complete extant collection of early Buddhist scriptures. It was passed down orally before finally being written down, in Pali, several centuries after the death of the Buddha. Also referred to as the *Tipitaka* ['Triple Basket', after the baskets for storing palm-leaf manuscripts], it consists of three divisions or baskets: the *Vinaya Pitaka*, *Sutta Pitaka*, and *Abhidhamma Pitaka*.

The Vinaya Pitaka, containing the rules of the *sangha*, is said to have been recited by Upali, one of the ten chief disciples, at the First Buddhist Council, convened shortly after the death of the Buddha. At the same gathering, Ananda, the Buddha's cousin, recited the Sutta Pitaka, consisting of the discourses and sermons of the Buddha and his close companions. For this reason, Ananda is known as the Treasurer of the Dhamma.

The Vinaya and Sutta Pitakas of the Pali Canon are very similar to the Vinaya and Sutta Pitakas of other Buddhist schools, in line with the contention that their contents predate the schisms. This, however, is not the case of the Abhidhamma ['Higher Teaching'] Pitaka, which contains more philosophical commentaries and treatises specific to the Theravadins.

The more than 10,000 sutras of the Sutta Pitaka are divided into five *nikayas* [collections]. The Khuddaka Nikaya includes the Dhammapada, a popular collection of sayings of the Buddha, as well as the largest collection of *jatakas*.

More popular even than the Dhammapada, and often illustrated in Buddhist architecture (Figure 15), are the *Jataka Tales*, a collection of stories from the previous lives of the Buddha. The *jatakas* ['birth stories'] are premised on the night of the Buddha's enlightenment, during which he remembered hundreds of thousands of former births.

In these past lives, he was not yet a Buddha, but a *bodhisattva*, which, in the Theravada tradition, is someone who has resolved to become a Buddha and received this confirmation or prediction from a living Buddha. Thus, in the *Jataka Tales*, the bodhisattva, having been inspired by his encounters with past Buddhas, makes a vow before the last Buddha Dipankara to himself become a Buddha by postponing his enlightenment until such a time as he be ready to teach others. He then spends many lives trying to fulfil this vow—supplying the material for the 547 jatakas in the Theravada collection. Maitreya, the next Buddha, will appear after the current Buddha's teachings and relics have disappeared from the world.

Figure 15. Northern gateway to the Great Stupa at Sanchi, carved with scenes from the Jataka Tales. First century BCE.

Whereas in the Theravada tradition, 'bodhisattva' usually refers to Shakyamuni ['the Sage of the Shakyas' i.e. the Buddha] and his previous incarnations, in the Mahayana tradition it refers less exclusively to anyone who has set out on the path to enlightenment and determined to teach that path to others.

The *Jataka Tales* are one of the oldest and largest collections of stories in the world, and the only one to trace the development of their central character over hundreds of births. Many of the tales are adapted from the immemorial fabularies of India and the world, often by replacing a character with the bodhisattva. Certain narratives pop up in the Hindu *Panchatantra* and even in *Æsop's Fables*: a variant of *The Tortoise and the Birds*, which features a tortoise dashed to pieces after falling from a great height, appears in all three collections. In the Indian versions, a tortoise who is grasping onto a stick carried between two geese falls for being too talkative; in the Greek version, he falls after asking an eagle to drop him so that he might learn to fly.

The earliest, verse stories, which would have been memorized for chanting, date to around the fifth century BCE. Many later tales, though in prose, contain elements of verse which may predate the prose. Shorter tales resemble the animal fables of Æsop; longer stories anticipate the Indian epics, which often draw upon them.

Each tale starts with a 'story from the present' involving a collection of persons in discussion with the Buddha. This prompts the telling of a 'story from the past', which, in most cases, sheds light on a problem from the present. Secondary characters are often the Buddha's disciples or prominent laypersons. Other recurrent characters are cousin Devadatta, generally appearing as a villain, and other members of Siddhartha's family. The cast in the story from the past interact to create trouble, with the bodhisattva character intervening to bring about a resolution. Each tale ends with a connection [*samodhana*], or 'who's who', in which the Buddha reveals who was who in the earlier life.

The bodhisattva features in all the tales, normally as the protagonist but occasionally as a minor character or observer. As well as a deva, a king, and an outcast, he is reincarnated as various animals, a tree spirit, a serpent king... His most frequent incarnation as a human being (in around a hundred lifetimes) is as an ascetic, followed by a king and king's advisor; as a deva, it is Indra; and as an animal, a monkey.

However, he is never incarnated as a woman or female. Although there are a few exceptions to prove the rule, women in the *Jataka Tales* are portrayed as devious schemers who lure men away from their higher calling.

All the tales are set in the Ganges basin. The most common setting for a story from the past is Kashi [Varanasi], and Taxila, in Gandhara, is often mentioned as a centre of learning.

In most tales, in whichever form he appears, the bodhisattva displays some virtue that the tale is intended to inculcate. In some stories, he behaves immorally. In one life, he is a thief [Jataka 318]; in another, a rich merchant who hires a high-class prostitute [Jataka 425]. More shockingly, as a crown prince banished with his brothers to the forest, he and his brothers kill and eat his sisters-in-law—leaving only the men, and his own wife, still alive [Jataka 193]. In other stories, he suffers karmic retribution for errors such as these, made in a previous life.

Over his lifetimes, the bodhisattva achieves several spiritual qualities, or 'perfections', that lead him to enlightenment and Buddhahood. Although no order is given, it is often taken that the last ten tales are his final lives-but-one, in which he arrives at the ten perfections, or *paramitas*: renunciation; resolution or determination; courage or diligence; patience; truthfulness; insight or wisdom; equanimity; morality; loving-kindness; and charity, generosity, or non-attachment.

Of these ten, rather long, 'Great Birth Stories', all named for their protagonist, the best known is the *Vessantara*, relating the bodhisattva's penultimate life as the generous-to-a-fault Prince Vessantara, who is banished by his father the king for giving away their rain-bringing white elephant to another, drought-plagued kingdom. Following his banishment, he goes with his family to live in the mountains, shedding all his possessions along the way, including, at last, his children and wife—who are later returned to him, along with the elephant, in time for his coronation. This story, which features on the gateways to the Great Stupa at Sanchi, is still celebrated in the Theravada heartlands of Sri Lanka, Thailand, Laos, Cambodia, and Myanmar with recitations, dance, theatre, and puppetry.

The parallels with Æsop are striking enough, but what is even more arresting, and curious, are the parallels with the Gospels.

For instance, in the Gospels, Jesus feeds a gathering of five thousand with five loaves and two fish; in Jataka 78, the Buddha feeds five hundred disciples with just a few cakes, and 'still there seemed no end to the cakes'.

In Jataka 190, a layman walks on water to reach the Buddha, but his feet begin to sink when, distracted by the waves, 'his ecstasy subsided'; at Matthew 14:28-31, Peter the Apostle walks on water to get to Jesus, but starts sinking when he begins to fear the wind. Jesus catches him, with the words, "O thou of little faith, wherefore didst thou doubt?"

12

THE PANCHATANTRA

The *Panchatantra* ['Five Principles, Treatises, or Books'], originally written in Sanskrit prose and verse, consists of an interwoven series of animal tales.

The preamble to the *Panchatantra*, which acts as an overarching frame, attributes the work to a Brahmin by the name of Vishnu Sharma, who may be no more than a literary invention or convention. The date of composition is unclear: 200 BCE might be a good guess, not least because many of the stories seem to be of Buddhist origin, with counterparts or correspondences in the *Jataka Tales*.

More important than any direct borrowing, the *Panchatantra* and *Jataka Tales* draw on a common store of ancient, preliterate folktales. Long after their composition, storytellers would have enriched their performances with music, mime, and dance, as well as a degree of improvisation or interpretation—as they still do today. The *Panchatantra* is replete with spare formulas such as 'he said' and 'he replied', suggesting a reliance on the narrator to extrapolate and express the appropriate emotions.

For all that, the *Panchatantra* has a much higher purpose than mere entertainment and histrionics. It is intended, at least notionally, as a *nitishastra*, that is, a textbook of *niti*—which might be translated as something like applied ethics or political science for princes and statesmen. As it aims at sound policy, *niti* is related to *artha*, or prosperity, which is one of the *purusharthas*, or aims of human life, alongside *dharma*, *kama*, and *moksha* (Chapter 8). The work's high aspirations are reflected in the subtitle of the 1480 Latin translation by John of Capua: *Directorium humanae vitae*, or *Guide for Human Life*.

Thus, the *Panchatantra* is in some sense allied to the *Arthashastra* (Chapter 17). Textual parallels have led some to speculate that Vishnu Sharma may be none other than Kautilya, the author of the *Arthashastra*, who also went by the name of Vishnugupta—although there is no evidence that Kautilya ever wrote a *nitishastra*.

Like the *Arthashastra*, the *Panchatantra* has been charged with qualified Machiavellianism. Unlike the *Jataka Tales*, or indeed, the fables of Æsop, it aims not at virtue but at worldly wisdom, with an emphasis on shrewdness and cleverness, which, in themselves, aim more at expediency than at morality. It is telling that, of the two jackals that run through the first treatise, the moralizing one, Karataka, is a mere sidekick who, in the end, loses out to Dhamanaka.

Still, *niti*, or sound policy, is a noble aim. The *Panchatantra* advocates restraint and moderation, and holds friendship in the highest regard. As per Aristotle, friendship is only possible between noble-minded equals who are 'cherished for their learning, refinement, and discipline' [II, 179].

In the preamble to the *Panchatantra*, it is related that King Sudarshan of Mahilaropya (a place unknown), despairing of his three sons, summoned the octogenarian Vishnu Sharma to his court. He petitioned the learned Brahmana to school the princes, within six months, in the art of government:

> Far better that a man have no sons born
> Or, that born they die; though there be grief, it passes soon;
> But, to have living sons, who turn out fools,
> And obstinate fools at that, that indeed
> Is a lifelong misery hard to bear.

King Sudarshan offered Vishnu Sharma a hundred land grants to take on the task—which he accepted, after refusing the land grants. Knowing that the task could not be accomplished by conventional means, he resorted to a succession of animal tales, which form the body of the *Panchatantra*.

Within this overarching frame story of the Brahmana schooling the three princes are five books or narratives, each with its own frame story. These secondary frame stories contain several overlapping stories, as one character narrates a story to the other, or others. An embedded story may contain further embedded stories, nesting in one another like Russian stacking dolls—making it quite easy, at least for this reader, to lose track of the plot. This is not unlike the *Mahabharata* (Chapter 20), which also makes heavy use of the 'story within a story', albeit on a much grander, epic scale.

The five books, or *tantras*, that make up the *Panchatantra* are entitled: *The Losing of Friends*; *The Winning of Friends*; *Of Crows and Owls*; *Loss of Gains*; and *Rash Deeds*. The first of the five books, featuring the pair of jackals, Karataka and Dhamanaka, makes up almost half of the entire work.

The last two books, which are very short, are more cautionary than advisory, and the fifth book is also unusual in featuring mostly human characters.

Although the narratives are in prose, the characters often turn to verse at heightened moments, or to make their point.

For example, one jackal tells the other:

> A hurricane does not uproot the pliant grass
> That bends low before its fury;
> It snaps only proud, lordly trees;
> A man of might lets his valour speak
> Only to others of equal might.

— I, 93

Also brought out in verse is a long diatribe against women, of which this is only a short selection:

> This whirlpool of suspicion, this mansion of immodesty,
> this city of audacity,
> This sanctuary of errors, this home of a hundred
> deceits, this field sown with doubts and distrust,
> This creature hard to tame even by the best, bulls
> among men, this casket entire of tricks—
> Who created this contraption called Woman? This
> nectar-coated poison? To set Virtue and the Law at
> naught?

— I, 142

Figure 16. Borzuy's Mission. Folio from a Kalilah wa Dimnah [Panchatantra] manuscript. Attributed to Gujarat, probably based on an Egyptian original. Second quarter of the sixteenth century. Metropolitan Museum of Art, New York.

In 570 CE, the original *Panchatantra* was translated from Sanskrit into Pahlavi, or Middle Persian, by the pre-eminent physician Borzuy.

According to Persia's national epic, the *Shahnameh*, or *Book of Kings* [31.3], Borzuy sought the permission of the emperor Khosrow I to travel to Hindustan in search of a mountain herb which, he had heard, could be sprinkled onto a corpse to bring it back to life (Figure 16).

Although Borzuy never found the mountain herb, a Kashmiri sage told him of a non-literal interpretation: the herb is wisdom, the mountain is learning, and the corpse is the man without knowledge. Having thus spoken, the sage pointed Borzuy to the *Panchatantra*.

Both Borzuy's translation and the original have been lost. In 750, Ibn al-Muqaffa translated the Borzuy into Arabic with some modifications, including the insertion of a moralizing chapter in which Dhamanaka is tried, found guilty, and sentenced to death. This Arabic translation, entitled *Kalilah wa Dimnah* after Karataka and Dhamanaka, still survives, as does a Syriac translation of the Borzuy.

Considered the first masterpiece of Arabic prose, *Kalilah wa Dimnah* became second only to the Koran in popularity, and strongly influenced the *Thousand and One Nights* [*Arabian Nights*]. It formed the basis of an eleventh century translation into Greek, entitled *Stephanites kai Ichnelates*, a twelfth century translation into Hebrew, and a thirteenth century translation into Old Castilian. The Hebrew translation, by Rabbi Joel, became the source of most other European translations, via the Latin translation of John of Capua, which, in 1480, became one of the earliest printed books.

In 1570, Sir Thomas North translated Anton Francesco Doni's Italian translation of the John of Capua as *The Fables of Bidpai: The Morall Philosophie of Doni*—'Bidpai' being a corruption of Vishnu Sharma, or Vidyapati in Sanskrit. And so it was that the *Panchatantra* arrived into English, as a sixth-degree translation of a work that had been travelling west, as well as north and southeast, for a thousand years.

The Fables of Bidpai became well known in the West, long before the Upanishads broke through. In the second edition of his *Fables* (1678), Jean de La Fontaine acknowledges that the greater part of his new material is 'derived from the Indian sage Pilpay'. In India, the *Hitopadesha* of Narayana (c. ninth century CE) borrows so heavily from the *Panchatantra* that nineteenth century Indologists attributed the work to Vishnu Sharma.

13

JAINISM, AHIMSA, AND GANDHI'S SATYAGRAHA

Ahimsa [non-injury, non-violence] runs through all Indian religions, and indeed all religions, but is at its most marked in Jainism. Today, there are around five million Jains, living mostly in India.

In Jain cosmology, the universe is eternal and uncreated—as is Jainism, which does not claim a historical founder. Time is cyclical, alternating between an ascending age (ascending towards purity) and a descending one, like our own. In every age, twenty-four great spiritual teachers, or *tirthankaras*, appear. A tirthankara, or 'ford-maker', having crossed the stream of interminable births and deaths, assists others in doing the same. In a descending age, the physical stature of both men and tirthankaras diminishes with the passing of time.

The first tirthankara of our age, Rishabhanatha, lived millions of years ago. The twenty-second tirthankara, Neminatha, a cousin of Krishna, lived around 85,000 years ago. The twenty-third tirthankara is a historical figure, Parshvanatha, who lived in the ninth, eighth, or seventh century BCE. And the twenty-fourth tirthankara is Vardhamana, also known as Mahavira or

Jina, a contemporary of the Buddha (Figure 17). The sign of Parshvanatha is the snake, and his colour is green; the sign of Vardhamana is the lion, and his colour is gold.

Like Parshvanatha, and the Buddha, Vardhamana is said to have been born to royalty, in Vaishali in modern-day Bihar. Vardhamana means 'prospering'—because the child seemed to bring good fortune. He grew up to be six-foot tall—tall, but not nearly as tall as Neminatha, who was 98-foot tall and lived for a thousand years.

At the age of thirty, Vardhamana, a second son, renounced his position to take up the life of a wandering mendicant. This vow was facilitated by the death of his parents, whom he had not wanted to displease. According to some accounts, he had by this time married and fathered a daughter.

On the ascetic path, Vardhamana was accompanied for a time by Goshala Maskariputra, who went on to establish the Ajivika movement. After twelve years of meditation and austerities, he achieved omniscience, or *kaivalya*, while sitting beneath a Sala tree on the banks of the Rijubalika. He then became known as Mahavira ['Great Hero'] and began to share his revelation. For having conquered his desires, he was given the title of Jina [Conqueror], which was then extended to other tirthankaras.

Mahavira, who may have been following in the path laid out by Parshvanatha, reformed Jainism into the religion that it has become, and organized his followers, known after him as Jains, into a four-fold order, namely, monk, nun, layman, and laywoman. Having renounced even the need for clothing, he went about naked, taking great care in his thirty years of wandering and preaching not to injure any form of life. He had eleven disciples known as the Ganadharas. Centuries later, his teachings, which had been passed down orally, were recorded in the Agamas.

Figure 17. Shrine with Four Jinas (Rishabhanatha, Neminatha, Parshvanatha, and Mahavira). Uttar Pradesh, c. 600 CE. Los Angeles County Museum of Art.

All forms of life have a soul or life force [*jiva*] that yearns for liberation from the cycle of rebirth and redeath. However, its liberation is impeded by its accumulated karma, conceived of as bits of material that cloud, pollute, and weigh upon it. *Arihants*, also known as *jinas* or *kevalins*, are perfected souls with a body but no karma; upon dying and shedding their body, they attain moksha and are then known as *siddhas* [liberated souls]. Because kevalins are free from desire and attachments, their energies are concentrated, so that they have unlimited *siddhis*, or spiritual powers. Most kevalins achieve no more than their own liberation, but a few go on to become thirthankaras, to teach others the path to salvation.

To liberate our soul, it is necessary to have right faith, right knowledge, and right conduct, and at the heart of right conduct are the five great vows: *Ahimsa*, *Satya* [Truthfulness], *Asteya* [Non-Stealing], *Aparigraha* [Non-Possession], and *Brahmacharya* [Chastity]. Non-possession encompasses property, relations, and emotions. The first four vows, or 'fourfold restraint', had already been established by Parshvanatha; to those four, Mahavira added the vow of celibacy. Even lay followers are required to observe the five vows, in so far as they are able to.

Mahavira set men and women on an equal footing; it is said that, at his death, the Jain community numbered 14,000 monks and 36,000 nuns. Still, being more rigid and less proselytizing, Jainism did not quite enjoy the success of Buddhism. Following a schism, the two major schools are the resident mendicant Shvetambara [White-Clad] and the wandering mendicant Digambara [Sky-Clad, i.e. naked]. Whereas the Shvetambaras hold the nineteenth tirthankara, Mallinatha, to have been a woman, the Digambaras reject this, claiming instead that women must be reborn as men before they can achieve kaivalya. Unsurprisingly, the Digambaras count many more monks than nuns. The Digambaras also reject many aspects of the story of Vardhamana/Mahavira.

Possibly, the 'naked gymnosophists' reportedly encountered by the Greek philosophers—the atomist Democritus of Abdera (d. c. 370 BCE) and the skeptic Pyrrho of Elis (d. c. 270 BCE)—on their eastern travels were, in fact, Digambara monks. Swayed, perhaps, by the radical skepticism of those other *shramanas*, the Ajnanas, Mahavira held that no philosophical point of view is the complete truth. This principle of *anekantavada* [many-sided reality] is illustrated by the parable of the elephant and five blind men. A strange animal is brought to town, and five blind men decide to go and inspect it in whatever way they can. The first, feeling the trunk, claims it is a snake; the second, grasping onto a tusk, claims it is a spear; the third, pulling on the tail, claims it is a rope; the fourth, hugging a leg, claims it is a tree trunk; while the fifth, having been slapped by an ear, feels sure that it is a fan. Whereas the Buddha with his Middle Way rejected the extremes of 'yes' and 'no', Mahavira included them both as a part of the truth: only a kevalin, who had achieved *kevala jnana* [omniscience], could comprehend a thing in its every aspect and manifestation.

But by far the most important Jain principle is the first of the five great vows, ahimsa. The motto *ahimsa paramo dharma* [non-violence is the highest virtue] decorates many a Jain temple. The most recognized Jain symbol is a raised hand with, on it, a dharmachakra, and within the dharmachakra, the word 'ahimsa' (Figure 18). Even eating honey is seen as violence to the bees that made it. Monks must take special precautions to avoid unintentionally harming a *jiva*, such as sweeping their path with a peacock-feather duster and not travelling during the rainy season. If you see a Jain monk wearing a mask, it is not because he is afraid of viruses.

There is a Jain story of a fire in the forest. To escape the fire, all the animals crowd around a lake. A restless elephant raises a leg, only for a rabbit to dart into the space beneath. So as not to harm the rabbit, the elephant holds up its leg for three days. Although it dies from the strain, it is reborn as a human being.

Many Jains abstain from farming, since agricultural operations are bound to injure small animals, including worms. However, violence in self-defence and war can be justified, for example, to protect Jain nuns, and there have been Jain monarchs and even Jain warriors. Non-violence has worked well for Jains, who are often stereotyped as wealthy merchants and bankers: perhaps ironically, Jains have come to form the wealthiest community in India.

Mahatma Gandhi extended the Jain principles of ahimsa and satya [truthfulness] into the political sphere as *satyagraha* ['holding onto truth']. This involves tackling injustice with non-violent resistance, truth telling, and conquering through conversion. Gandhi practised satyagraha not only in the Indian Independence Movement but also, in its embryonic form, during his earlier struggles for Indian rights in South Africa. In a letter, he distinguished it from passive resistance in three points: it is a weapon of the strong; it admits of no violence under any circumstance whatsoever; and it ever insists upon truth. Satyagraha influenced Martin Luther King, Jr. (MLK) during the Civil Rights Movement and Nelson Mandela in his struggle against apartheid. MLK went so far as to call Gandhi 'the greatest Christian of the modern world'. Gandhi looked upon ahimsa and satya as two sides of the same coin: truth leads to non-violence, just as non-violence leads to truth. The means, he said, should be as pure as the end.

An uncommon Jain practice that has attracted attention is *sallekhana*, in which a person whose body is no longer serving him invites death by voluntarily reducing his intake of food and drink. There are several variants of sallekhana, including one in which the person remains immobile, and the process can last from a few days to several years. Sallekhana is regarded by Jains as a means of thinning the passions and destroying karma before death. But in 2015, the Rajasthan High Court banned the practice, which it assimilated to suicide—though Jains argue that, unlike suicide, sallekhana is not an act of passion, and does not involve poisons or violence. In 2016, the Supreme Court of India lifted the ban, and in 2017 the Indian parliament in any case decriminalized suicide.

Figure 18. The Jain ahimsa hand, with raised hand for 'stop' and a dharmachakra with the word 'ahimsa' in its centre.

Buddhism and Jainism arose, in part, from a rejection of the Vedic blood sacrifice, and served in turn to accelerate the shift towards vegetarianism, and theism. The ritual did not die, but was transformed, with *yagna* replaced by *puja*, in which the sacrifice is symbolic, with fruits, flowers, and incense offered in lieu of animals. But whereas yagna was a means of effecting an end, puja was merely a means of propitiating the gods, who had taken control over human affairs, or, at least, set themselves up as middlemen.

Buddhism and Jainism were not the only reformist shramana movements. At some point, Vardhamana parted ways with his friend, Goshala Maskariputra, who went on to establish the rival Ajivika movement. As the Ajivika scriptures have been lost, the only information about them comes from partial Buddhist and Jain sources. It seems that the Ajivikas believed in an impersonal cosmic principle called *niyati* [fate, destiny], meaning that they embraced determinism and rejected the free will implied by karma theory. But although they did not believe that their actions had karmic consequences, still they continued to practise austerities—presumably because they thought them inherently worthwhile. The Ajivikas reached the height of their influence under Ashoka's father, Bindusara, who may have patronised them, and are mentioned in Ashoka's Seventh Pillar Edict. By the fourteenth century, their movement had completely died out.

If you think the Ajivikas were out on a limb, wait until you hear about the Charvakas, who had much in common with the Ajnanas, or radical skeptics, for example, in arguing for the futility of metaphysical speculation. Founded, possibly, by Brihaspati, author of the lost *Brihaspatisutra*, the Charvakas held that direct perception is the only means of establishing any truth, and that matter—in the form of air, earth, fire, and water—is all that exists. Thus, they rejected the supernatural, including the soul, karma, reincarnation, and all religion: the elements by combination give rise to consciousness, just like molasses by fermentation acquire the power of intoxication. Instead of liberation, the ethical goal is to pursue individual pleasure while avoiding pain. As far from the Brahmanas and the Jains as it is possible to imagine, the Charvakas anticipated the Greek hedonists Aristippus of Cyrene and Epicurus of Samos. In India, they created the climate in which works such as the *Arthashastra* and *Kama Sutra* could be written, and laid the ground for empirical inquiry and the Gupta Golden Age. Later also known, derogatorily, as Lokayata ['the philosophy of the people'], Charvaka died out in the twelfth century.

14

THE MAURYAS: CHANDRAGUPTA AND ASHOKA

By the fourth century BCE, the Kingdom of Magadha, with its capital at Pataliputra [modern-day Patna, in Bihar], had grown pre-eminent among India's assorted kingdoms and republics.

The Nandas had overthrown the Shaishunagas to become the fifth ruling dynasty of Magadha, and expanded the empire to include much of central, eastern, and north-eastern India.

According to the historian Plutarch (d. 119 CE), the ninth Nanda emperor, Dhana Nanda (d. 321 BCE), could call upon 200,000 infantry, 80,000 cavalry, 8,000 chariots, and 6,000 fighting elephants. So great are the numbers that Plutarch feels the need to specify that he is not exaggerating. The first century historian Quintus Curtius Rufus also quotes 200,000 infantry, although fewer cavalry, chariots, and elephants.

When Alexander the Great invaded India in 326 BCE, bringing disorder to the Punjab and northwest, his men mutinied at the prospect of crossing the Hyphasis River [modern-day Beas River] and facing Dhana Nanda's massive army.

Plutarch claims that a young Sandrocottus [Chandragupta] met with Alexander, and that Chandragupta often remarked in later times that, had he tried, Alexander could easily have conquered India on account of Dhana Nanda's unpopularity with the people [*Life of Alexander* 62].

The origins of Chandragupta Maurya are obscure. By some accounts, he was born into a family left destitute by the death of his father, and grew up among herdsmen, hunters, or peacock tamers. By other accounts, he was a spurned relative of Dhana Nanda—or presumed relative, if it is true that Nanda was, as claimed by Curtius, the son of a handsome barber [*History of Alexander* 9.2.4-10].

In any case, Chandragupta was picked up by the Brahmana politician Kautilya [also called Chanakya], author of the *Arthashastra*, who mentored him and sent him to Taxila to complete his education. However humble his origins, it seems unlikely that Kautilya would have noticed Chandragupta, still less favoured him, had he not been a Kshatriya.

Having lived through the turmoil created by Alexander, Kautilya wished to establish durable peace and prosperity in India, and the clearest way of doing this was to take over the throne of Magadha. In addition, Kautilya had a terrible opinion of Dhana Nanda, who, it is said, called him ugly and banished him from court. Thus, the political mastermind decided to supplant Dhana Nanda with the much more capable and malleable Chandragupta.

After Taxila, Chandragupta gathered a mercenary army and popular support, while Kautilya worked behind the scenes to raise funds and build bridges with politicians and courtiers. Chandragupta began by conquering outlying Nanda territories before, in around 324 BCE (the date is disputed), seizing the Magadha capital of Pataliputra.

Now in control of Magadha's unrivalled army and resources, Chandragupta set about expanding his territories. And so it was, in a story that is rarely told, that Alexander, a Macedonian, led to the creation of the first pan-Indian empire.

When Alexander died, far away in Babylon, in 323 BCE, the Greek satrapies that he had established in northwest India became easy pickings for Chandragupta.

In 305, Seleucus I Nicator, the successor of Alexander in the East and founder of the Seleucid Empire, attempted to retake the Punjab, only to be pushed back by Chandragupta.

In 303, the two emperors reached an agreement, sealed by a marriage (it is not clear who married whom), wherein Seleucus ceded Arachosia [Kandahar], Gedrosia [Balochistan], and Paropamisadae [Gandhara] to Chandragupta in exchange for peace, prosperity, and five hundred war elephants which he deployed to defeat his great western rival, Antigonus I Monophthalmos [the One-Eyed], at the Battle of Ipsus.

Seleucus also sent several Greeks, including an ambassador, Megasthenes, to the Mauryan court at Pataliputra. The *Indica* of Megasthenes, of which only fragments survive, is the first written account of India by a Westerner. In it, Megasthenes marvels at the wealth of India and the opulence of the Mauryan court, but is uncritical in reporting accounts of giant gold-digging ants, a race of men with no mouths, and ear-sleepers with ears so large that they are used as blankets.

Now in control of an empire stretching from Balochistan to Bengal, Chandragupta established a central administration inspired by that of the Persian Achaemenid Empire and patterned along the lines of Kautilya's *Arthashastra* (Chapter 17).

He charged his officials with building roads, reservoirs, ports, mines, armouries, and other infrastructure. He set up a 'Board of Works' for the upkeep of the Royal Road that ran, over more than a thousand miles, from Pataliputra to Taxila. According to Megasthenes, he appointed officers to ensure that no foreigner be wronged—fostering a climate of tolerance that enabled minority movements such as Buddhism and Jainism to thrive.

Having overthrown Dhana Nanda, Chandragupta and Kautilya took great precautions to secure the reign and protect against assassination. Megasthenes relates that Chandragupta only left his palace for prescribed purposes such as administering justice and offering sacrifice. When out hunting on elephant back, he was surrounded by a female bodyguard mounted on horses, chariots, and elephants. The custom of a female royal bodyguard, deemed to be less susceptible to intrigues, perdured into the Gupta era (319-550 CE).

In 297, at the height of his power, Chandragupta did the greatest thing that an emperor can do: abdicate in favour of philosophy. In this, he had been influenced by the omniscient Jain Bhadrabahu, who had foreseen the onset of a twelve-year famine. Leaving the empire in the charge of his son Bindusara, he travelled with a congregation of monks to Shravanabelagola in Karnataka, Southern India, where he lived for several years as an ascetic before submitting to *sallekhana* (Chapter 13) and fasting to death.

Bindusara took in the region of Mysore, expanding his father's empire across the Deccan. At court, Megasthenes was succeeded by Deimachos of Plateia, who represented the successor of Seleucus, Antiochus I Soter, to Bindusara.

According to the third century *Deipnosophistae* of Athenaeus, Bindusara asked Antiochus to send him sweet wine, dried figs, and a sophist—suggesting a desire in Bindusara to learn Greek philosophy. Antiochus replied: 'We shall send you the wine and the figs, but in Greece the laws forbid a sophist to be sold.'

When Bindusara died in c. 273, he was succeeded, following a struggle, by his son Ashoka, who held all but the far south of the subcontinent—a feat not to be repeated until the reign of the Mughal emperor Aurangzeb (d. 1707).

According to the *Pratisarga Parva* of the *Bhavishya Purana*, 'Chandragupta married with a daughter of Suluva [Seleucus], the Yavana [Greek] king of Pausasa. Thus, he mixed the Buddhists and the Yavanas. He ruled for 60 years. From him, Vindusara was born and ruled for the same number of years as his father. His son was Ashoka.'

This account, although contradicted by other accounts, raises the possibility that Ashoka was at least a quarter Greek.

For all that he left behind, the name of Ashoka ['Without sorrow', pronounced 'Ashoke'] had almost been forgotten. In 1837, the orientalist James Prinsep deciphered the Brahmi script, and it became apparent that the Ashoka named as a Mauryan king in the Puranas corresponded with the Devampiya Piyadassi ['Beloved of the Gods, Fair of Face'] referred to on several ancient rock and pillar edicts.

Bindusara sent Ashoka, probably his second son, to Taxila to suppress a rebellion. Having proven himself in Taxila, Ashoka received the governorship of Ujjain. In Vidisha, on the road to Ujjain, he fell in love with a merchant's daughter, Devi, whom he did not marry, but who bore him a son, Mahinda, and a daughter, Sanghamitta.

When Bindusara died, Ashoka, who was more popular with court officials, the army, and the people, proclaimed himself emperor over his elder half-brother, Crown Prince Sushima. In an unlikely story, he had 99 of his half-brothers killed, sparing only his uterine brother Vitashoka.

In those early days, he became known as Chandashoka, or Ashoka the Cruel. According to Buddhist chroniclers keen to emphasize his then brutality, he had five hundred concubines burnt alive for calling him ugly and built a torture house that came to be known as Ashoka's Hell.

In 260 BCE, eight years after his coronation, he conquered the prosperous kingdom of Kalinga [roughly, modern Odisha, to the south of Patna/Pataliputra], resulting in the slaughter of 100,000, the deportation of 150,000, and the loss of many more to famine and disease.

Gripped by remorse, he underwent a transformation, renouncing armed conquest and converting to 'the Dhamma', his political adaptation of Buddhism. From then on, he modelled himself on a Buddhist chakravartin, a universal monarch who derives his authority from dharma and the rule of righteousness.

To spread dharma, he inscribed edicts on rocks and pillars throughout his empire, at pilgrimage sites, along trade routes, and in border cities. 28 inscriptions have been found, classified according to size and medium: 14 Major Rock Edicts, 3 Minor Rock Edicts, 7 Major Pillar Edicts, and 4 Minor Pillar Edicts.

In Major Rock Edict 13, he himself tells us:

> Beloved of the Gods, King Piyadasi, conquered the Kalingas eight years after his coronation. A hundred and fifty thousand were deported, a hundred thousand were killed, and many more died. Having defeated the Kalingas, Beloved of the Gods came to feel a strong inclination towards the Dhamma, a love for the Dhamma and for instruction in Dhamma. Now Beloved of the Gods feels deep remorse for having conquered the Kalingas ... the killing, death, or deportation of a hundredth, or even a thousandth part of those who died during the conquest of Kalinga now pains Beloved of the Gods... Now it is conquest by Dhamma that Beloved of the Gods considers to be the best conquest.

Most of the inscriptions are in Prakrit, in the Brahmi script, although those in the northwest are in Greek or Aramaic [the *lingua franca* of Persia]. The pillars, of which 19 have been found, are carved from a single stone, and may be as high as 15 metres and as heavy as 50 tonnes. They are crowned by a lion or bull sitting or standing on an inverted lotus, and finished in the characteristic Mauryan polish. The famous Lion Capital (Figures 8 & 19), with four lions representing the Four Noble Truths, surmounted the Sarnath Pillar (Minor Pillar Edict 2), excavated by the Archaeological Survey of India in the early years of the twentieth century.

In Major Rock Edict 8, Ashoka proclaims that, ten years after his coronation, he went on a 'Dhamma tour', teaching the Dhamma, giving out gold, and visiting the Bodhi Tree at Bodh Gaya—whereas 'in the past kings went out on pleasure tours during which there was hunting and other entertainment'. He appointed Dhamma officials to teach the Dhamma and dispatched Dhamma embassies to distant lands, including China, Southeast Asia, the Greek kingdoms, and Sri Lanka, where his son and daughter, Mahinda and Sanghamitta, went to live as monk and nun. He built many monasteries and stupas (although the quoted number of 84,000 stupas is doubtless an exaggeration) and divided the Buddha's relics between them. In 250, in an attempt at doctrinal unity, he convened and attended the Third Buddhist Council at Pataliputra. By metamorphosing from Chandashoka to Dharmashoka, he transformed Buddhism from a marginal movement into a world religion.

Ashoka was religious without being fanatical, at once devout and oecumenical. In Major Rock Edict 7, he reasons that 'all religions should reside everywhere, for all of them desire self-control and purity of heart'. In Major Rock Edict 12, he cautions that 'whoever praises his own religion from excessive devotion, and condemns others with the thought, 'Let me glorify my own religion,' only harms his own religion.'

And he can be disarmingly candid, like here in the Separate Kalinga Rock Edicts:

> All men are my children. What I desire for my own children, and I desire their welfare and happiness both in this world and the next, that I desire for all men. You do not understand to what extent I desire this, and if some of you do understand, you do not understand the full extent of my desire.

Sincere or not, it is great propaganda. Ashoka thought that by projecting a model of enlightened government, neighbouring territories would be drawn into his empire, forming a kind of enlightened confederacy not to be seen again until the advent, more than two thousand years later, of the European Union.

Ashokan reforms included abolishing the death penalty, prohibiting animal sacrifice, and restricting meat consumption. In Major Rock Edict 1, he declares, against the Brahmanas, that 'no living beings are to be slaughtered or offered in sacrifice':

Figure 19. The Lion Capital of Ashoka. Sarnath Museum. Photo: Chrisi1964. CC BY 4.0 (slightly cropped).

> Formerly, in the kitchen of Beloved of the Gods, King Piyadasi, hundreds of thousands of animals were killed every day to make curry. But now ... only three creatures, two peacocks and a deer, are killed, and the deer not always. And in time, not even these three creatures will be killed.

In Pillar Edict 5, Ashoka prohibits the killing of 'all four-footed creatures that are neither useful nor edible', as well as bulls, deer, and certain birds and fish. He founded hospitals for humans and animals, and imported medicinal herbs that could not be grown in sufficient quantities. Along the highways, he built rest houses, dug wells, and planted mango groves.

Ashoka's palace at Pataliputra, modelled after the Achaemenid palace at Persepolis, marked the beginning of stone building in India, and, likely, it is also from Darius that he took the idea for the edicts—although his were a lot more subtle, and successful, in extolling his greatness.

Tivala is the only son mentioned by name in the edicts. However, when Ashoka died in 232, in his seventies, he was succeeded, it seems, by a grandson, Dasharatha, who struggled to hold on to the empire. In 185, the Mauryan Empire was succeeded by the Shunga Empire after the ninth and last Mauryan emperor, Brihadratha, was murdered by a general, Pushyamitra Shunga, during a military parade.

For all the glories of the Guptas (Chapter 23), India would not be reunited for another two thousand years.

15

GREEK INDIA

The decline of the Mauryas, and their downfall in 185 BCE, left the Khyber Pass unguarded, inviting a Greek invasion of Northwest India.

By this time, the Greeks and the Indians had already had a long relationship. The Greeks referred to the Indians as the *Indoi*, while the Indians referred to the Greeks as the *Yavanas* [which may be a transliteration of 'Ionian']—a term that they later extended to all foreigners.

In the *Strategemata* [13.4], the military historian Polyænus (fl. 160 CE) claims that the Greek hero Herakles [Hercules] fathered a daughter, Pandaie, in India, and established her as an Indian queen.

In Greek myth, Dionysus, the god of wine and dissolution, travels as far east as India to escape from Hera. According to the historian Diodorus Siculus (d. 30 BCE), 'the most ancient Dionysus was an Indian ... [who] visited with an army all the inhabited world and gave instruction both as to the culture of the vine and the crushing of the clusters in the wine-vats...'

In 533 BCE, Cyrus the Great, the founder of the Achaemenid Persian Empire, crossed the Hindu Kush and took tribute from the cities of the Indus. In 490, on the other side of their vast territory, his successor Darius the Great almost succeeded in capturing Athens. In the foundation tablets of the Apadana [Audience Hall] in Persepolis, Darius describes himself as ruler of an empire stretching 'from the Sacae who are beyond Sogdia to Kush, and from Sind to Lydia'. In 480, his son Xerxes came back for Athens, desecrating the Acropolis and burning the city to the ground. It is into this charred landscape that, in 470, Socrates would be born.

The Achaemenids had a custom of relocating rebellious Greek communities to the other, Indian, extremity of their empire. For example, after the sack of the Libyan Greek colony of Barca in 515, Darius resettled some of the captives in a village in Bactria —so that when Alexander arrived in 329, Bactria already had a long-established Greek community.

In 331, Alexander had conquered the Persian Empire, leaving the emperor Darius III to flee, and later be assassinated by his own officials. In 328, Alexander sought to secure his line of communications so as to proceed into India proper. He invited the chieftains of the former satrapy of Gandhara to submit to him, and subdued those who refused to do so in the so-called Cophen campaign (327-326).

In 326, Alexander crossed the Hindu Kush into the Punjab and defeated the Indian king Porus in the Battle of the Hydaspes—'Hydaspes' being the Greek name for the Jhelum, a tributary of the Chenab and Indus. The tall and handsome Porus, mounted on a great elephant, fought to the bitter end, so impressing Alexander that he spared his life, made him a satrap, and extended his dominion.

More valiant still, according to Plutarch, was Porus' elephant:

> [The beast] showed remarkable intelligence and solicitude for the king, bravely defending him and beating back his assailants while he was still in full vigour, and when it perceived that its master was worn out with a multitude of missiles and wounds, fearing he should fall off, it knelt softly on the ground, and with its proboscis gently took each spear and drew it out of his body.

Alexander too had fought fearlessly, and his ageing horse Bucephalus, whom he had ridden down the Nile and across Asia, died from its battle wounds. Alexander founded two cities on either side of the Hydaspes, naming one Nicaea [Victory] and the other Alexandria Bucephalous in honour of the horse that only he, as a mere twelve-year-old, had been able to tame.

Now intent on crossing the Ganges, Alexander marched his men eastward. But upon reaching the Hyphasis [modern-day Beas River], which marked the border with the Nanda Empire, his depleted troops, exhausted after years of campaigning and intimidated by the combined might of the Nanda army and monsoonal Ganges, refused to go any further.

Once he had accepted this, Alexander turned south, downriver, to delimit and secure the eastern border of his empire—suffering a near-fatal injury during the conquest of Malhi.

The turning at the Hyphasis is one the great 'what if' moments in the history of Greece, India, and the world. Had his men not mutinied, or had he sat down with Chandragupta or Kautilya, Alexander may very well have conquered India—as later claimed by Chandragupta (Figure 20).

On the march south, some time after Malhi, the convalescent Alexander captured and questioned ten troublesome gymnosophists ['naked philosophers', possibly Jain Digambara monks]—as related by Plutarch:

He captured ten of the gymnosophists who had ... made the most trouble for the Macedonians. These philosophers were reputed to be clever and concise in answering questions, and Alexander therefore put difficult questions to them, declaring that he would put to death him who first made an incorrect answer, and then the rest, in an order determined in like manner, and he commanded one of them, the oldest, to be the judge in the contest. The first one, accordingly, being asked which, in his opinion, were more numerous, the living or the dead, said that the living were, since the dead no longer existed. The second, being asked whether the earth or the sea produced larger animals, said the earth did, since the sea was but a part of the earth. The third, being asked what animal was the most cunning, said: "That which up to this time man has not discovered." The fourth, when asked why he had induced Sabbas to revolt, replied, "Because I wished him to either live nobly or die nobly." The fifth, being asked which, in his opinion, was older, day or night, replied, "Day, by one day;" and he added, upon the king expressing amazement, that hard questions must have hard answers. Passing on, then, to the sixth, Alexander asked how a man could be most loved: "If" said the philosopher, "he is most powerful, and yet does not inspire fear." Of the three remaining, he who was asked how one might become a god instead of a man, replied, "By doing something which a man cannot do;" the one who was asked which was the stronger, life or death, answered, "Life, since it supports so many ills." And the last, asked how long it were well for a man to live, answered, "Until he does not regard death as better than life." So then, turning to the judge, Alexander bade him give his opinion. The judge declared that they had answered one worse than another. "Well, then" said Alexander, "thou shalt die first for giving such a verdict." "That cannot be" said the judge, "unless thou falsely saidst that thou wouldst put to death first him who answered worst."

Figure 20. Silver tetradrachm with an observe portrait of Alexander wearing an elephant scalp complete with trunk and tusks. Ptolemy issued these coins after hijacking Alexander's body and enshrining it in a magnificent mausoleum in Alexandria. They hark back to Alexander's own coins, on which he sports the head of the Nemean lion.

In 324, with Alexander barely out of India, Chandragupta did what Alexander could not and overthrew Dhana Nanda, in all likelihood, with the help of Greek mercenaries, who would have marched into the Magadhan capital of Pataliputra. Magadha formed the core of India's ancient empires, including the Nanda, Maurya, Shunga, and Gupta Empires.

After Alexander's untimely death in 323, his Indian satrapies became vulnerable to Chandragupta.

After much plotting and intrigue, the vast Asian section of Alexander's empire fell into the control of the Macedonian general Seleucus, who, as Seleucus I Nicator ['Victor'], founded the Seleucid Empire.

In 305, Seleucus invaded the region of the Indus in a bid to retake Alexander's Indian satrapies, only to be checked by Chandragupta. The so-called Seleucid-Mauryan War, which may not have been a war, or a hot war, came to a resolution in 303, when the overextended Seleucus reached an agreement with Chandragupta: Seleucus would clear out of India and cede further territory to Chandragupta, in exchange for stability in the East and 500 war elephants to deploy—successfully, as it turned out—against his Greek rivals in the West (Figure 21).

The Greeks that had settled in now Mauryan lands cohabited and integrated with the Indians, so well that many followed Ashoka in converting to Buddhism. Ashoka embraced them in return: one of his emissaries was a Greek Buddhist monk by the name of Dharmarakshita ['Protected by Dharma'].

Many years later, in around 250 BCE, the satrap of Bactria, Diodotus, seceded from the Seleucid Empire to become Diodotus I Soter ['Saviour'].

In 186 BCE, around the time of the overthrow of the Mauryas, the Greco-Bactrian king Demetrius I Anicetus ['Unconquered'] invaded India, perhaps to support the Mauryas, or to protect Greek populations from persecution by the Shungas, or for naked gain. The areas of India that he conquered seceded from Bactria to form the Indo-Greek Kingdom, or Yavanaraja.

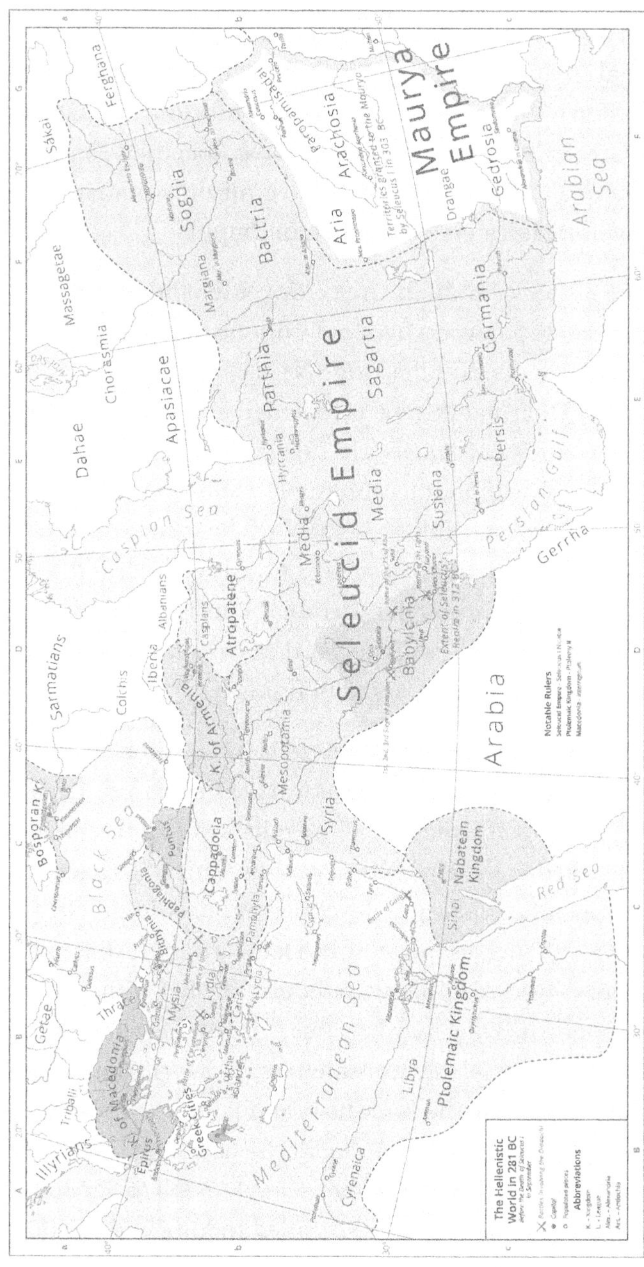

Figure 21. The Hellenistic World in 281 BCE, showing Bactria and the territories ceded by Seleucus to Chandragupta. Credit: Cattette. CC BY 4.0.

This new entity was seldom if ever cohesive, with several regional capitals like Taxila, Pushkalavati, and Sagala, and a succession of more than thirty often conflicting kings. Still, the Indo-Greek Kingdom outlived the Greco-Bactrian Kingdom, which, in 120 BCE, fell to the Greater Yuezhi, a nomadic horde that later organized into the Kushan Empire.

The most successful Indo-Greek king, Menander I Soter (d. 130 BCE), became a famous figure of Buddhism. His purported dialogue with the Buddhist sage Nagasena, said to have been a student of Dharmarakshita, is recorded in the *Milinda Panha* [*Questions of King Menander*]. In this lively dialogue, Nagasena makes use of metaphor to illuminate philosophical problems such as how karma and samsara might be able to operate in the absence of an Atman. Nagasena famously compares the self to a chariot, which, although functional, consists of no more than the sum of its aggregates [*skandhas*]. Having been persuaded by Nagasena, Milinda converts to Buddhism.

This high degree of cultural syncretism can still be admired in the Greco-Buddhist, or Gandhara, art of the period. The Greek influence is already present in the pillars of Ashoka, and is even more marked in the Pataliputra capital, which has been dated to the reign of Ashoka and described as quasi-Ionic. Greek philosophers such as the atomist Democritus of Abdera and the skeptic Pyrrho of Elis, who reportedly met with gymnosophists [Diogenes Laertius 9.7, 9.11], may have been influenced by *shramana* movements such as Jainism, Ajnana, and Charvaka. Like the Buddhists and Jains, the Epicureans and Stoics had a lot to say about desire as the cause of suffering. In around 10 CE, the Indo-Greek Kingdom fell to Scythian tribes from Central Asia, the so-called Indo-Scythians, but Greek populations remained in India for several more centuries before being completely assimilated—leaving nothing behind but books, art, and the occasional pair of green eyes.

16

DHARMA, THE LAWS OF MANU, AND THE CASTE SYSTEM

Gandhi's *satyagraha* was guided by dharma, and the wheel of dharma features on the Indian flag. But what, exactly, is dharma? In Chapter 8, I defined dharma briefly as 'duty'. In truth, dharma cannot so easily be translated into English and, even in India, means several things.

'Dharma' derives from the Sanskrit *dhr*, to hold, support, or sustain. In the Vedas, it refers to behaviours and rituals that accord with cosmic law and order, or *rita*. By extension, it comes to signify 'right conduct', 'virtue', 'piety', 'custom', and 'duty'—to oneself, one's ancestors, society, nature, and future generations. Thus, it is justice in its broadest sense. When dharma is strong, society flourishes, but when it decays, human life descends to what Kautilya calls *matsya nyaya*, 'the law of the fish', that is, the law of the jungle [1.4.13-14].

In the Kandahar Bilingual Rock Inscription, Ashoka translates 'dharma' into Greek as *eusebeia*, that is, duty and reverence to the gods, the state, and one's parents, or, more broadly, right relations relative to one's station. *Eusebeia* is akin, also, to the Roman concept of *pietas*.

In the Great Forest Upanishad, Yajnavalkya says that there is nothing higher than dharma, which he equates to truth [*satya*] and righteousness [1.4.14]. Thus, the opposite of dharma is not merely *adharma* but *maya*.

Dharma is, of course, one of the three, and later four, *purusharthas*, or aims of human life, along with *artha*, *kama*, and *moksha* (Chapter 8). Dharma prevails over artha and kama, and, since one could hardly arrive at moksha without dharma, may be held to prevail over moksha as well.

Artha is important not only in itself, but also in supporting dharma and kama. In times of poverty and insecurity, it becomes harder to abide by dharma. A vicious circle takes hold, wherein adharma leads to greater distress, which leads, in turn, to greater adharma.

In Buddhism, 'the dharma' [*dhamma* in Pali and Prakrit] also refers to the teachings of the Buddha, especially the Four Noble Truths. Alongside the Buddha and the Sangha, it is one of the Three Jewels [*Triratna*] of Buddhism (Chapter 11).

In Hinduism, a distinction is made between *sanatana dharma*, or 'eternal law', incumbent on everyone, and *svadharma*, or one's own duty as determined by one's qualities, propensities, occupation, caste, and stage of life [*ashrama*].

The conflict between these two dharmas is one of the principal themes of the *Bhagavad Gita*, in which Arjuna hesitates between his svadharma as a warrior and the general injunction not to harm or kill. Krishna's response is that, in such cases, svadharma ought to prevail.

It might be said that the claimed superiority of the Brahmanas resides in that their svadharma perfectly coincides with the universal dharma: because a conflict never arises, they never need to compromise their ethics, that is, sully themselves.

The *Mahabharata*, of which the *Bhagavad Gita* is a part, presents three broad approaches to moral problems, embodied by Bhima (brute force, ego, or desire), Yudhisthira (rigid moral law), and Arjuna (moral indeterminacy), who, wavering between the paths of his two elder brothers, is forced to make difficult, existential choices (Chapters 20 & 21).

These three moral approaches might be compared to Kierkegaard's three types of life: the aesthetic life, the ethical life, and the religious life, which, for Kierkegaard, is the highest type of life. In deferring to universal moral principles while also attending to particularities, the religious life opens the door to moral indeterminacy, that is, to ambiguity, uncertainty, and anxiety, or 'fear and trembling':

> Wherefore, my beloved, as ye have always obeyed, not as in my presence only, but now much more in my absence, work out your own salvation with fear and trembling.
>
> — PHILIPPIANS 2:12 (KJV)

Notions of svadharma abound in Plato's *Republic*, in which the three-tiered social order of the ideal republic is reinforced by a 'useful lie', the co-called myth of the metals. In Book 6, Plato says that the rare person who has made it into the light of the sun has a duty to return into the cave and muddy himself in the menial matters of men, because the state aims at the happiness not of a single escapee but of all its citizens.

The Stoics, too, held that we must play our part as skilfully and artfully as we can, without regard for the outcome, hence the metaphor of the Stoic archer, who, having decided on the target, focuses on the shooting, which is in his control, rather than on the striking, which is not.

Life, says the Stoic teacher Epictetus (d. 135 CE), is like a ball game: if we start caring about the ball more than the game, it is no longer a game but a brawl, and no fun at all. The important thing is not to hog the ball, or even to win, but to play and enjoy the best game we can [*Discourses* II, 5.15-20].

In his diary or notebook, now known as the *Meditations*, Marcus Aurelius (d. 180 CE) peps himself for the burdens of the purple:

> At dawn, when you struggle to get out of bed, tell yourself, 'I have to go to work—as a human being. Of what do I have to complain, if I'm going to do what I was born for—the things I was brought into the world to do? Or is this what I was made for? To huddle under the blankets and stay warm?' [5.1]

For the Stoics, to embrace life is to embrace fate, which is to embrace God and be at one with the *logos*. To put this in Indian or Hindu terms, it is to be at one with *rita* and Brahman, and thereby to achieve *moksha*, which is liberation from *maya*, *dukkha*, and *samsara*.

At the end of the *Mahabharata*, the Pandavas set off for Mount Meru. They fall one by one along the way, so that Yudhisthira arrives at the gates of heaven with only their dog. Indra invites him in, but refuses to admit the dog. Yudhisthira turns away, saying that he cannot abandon his faithful companion. At this, the dog reveals himself as Yama, also known as Dharma, who informs Yudhisthira that this was his final test.

Whereas the Vedas, down to the Upanishads, are considered as revealed texts [*shruti*, 'that which has been heard'], later works which emerged out of the shruti literature are considered as remembered texts [*smriti*, 'that which has been remembered']. Shruti texts are the more authoritative, for having been given by God, and received by sages in visions and voices.

Smriti texts include the Shastras, the Puranas, and the Itihasas [histories, or verse epics]. The principal theme of the two greatest Itihasas, the *Ramayana* and *Mahabharata*, is dharma. Over time, dharma decays, leading to destruction or the arrival of a restorer, or avatar. Whereas the *Ramayana* is set in Treta Yuga, the second of the four yugas in the current time cycle, the *Mahabharata* is set in Dvapara Yuga, the third yuga. Thus, as we shall see (Chapters 19 & 20), the evil in the *Mahabharata* is greater than that in the *Ramayana*.

In ancient times, the Vedic schools preserved their teachings on dharma in collections of *sutras*, or aphorisms: the *dharmasutras*, concerned with sacred laws and customs, and the *grihyasutras*, concerned with domestic ceremonies. Over time, some of these sutras came to be compiled, expanded, and versified. Of these *dharmashastras*, the *Manava Dharmashastra*, also known as the *Manusmriti* or *Laws of Manu*, became pre-eminent.

Multiple versions of the *Manava Dharmashastra* are extant, as well as nine complete commentaries. The work probably dates to circa 100 CE, although some of its contents may be several centuries older. Even if it did have a single author or compiler, it would have been subject to revision by later authors—helping to explain the many contradictions within.

In search of a legal basis for governing the Hindu population within their jurisdiction, the East India Company misconstrued the *Manava Dharmashastra* as a code of law and called it the *Laws of Manu*. In fact, laws are only a small part of the work, which, in all probability, never served, wholesale, as a code of law. Instead, the work presents a Brahmanical ideal of Hindu society, outlining the ritual and social obligations of all Hindus according to gender, caste, and stage of life.

Although *Manava* is thought to allude to the ancient Manava school, the name led to the work being attributed to Manu, the mythical first man. 'Manu' derives from the Sanskrit *manas* [mind, spirit], and ultimately from the Proto-Indo-European root **men-* [to think]—from which are derived a great number of English words, including 'dementia', 'mania', 'mantic', 'mantra', 'mental', 'muse', 'music', and even, perhaps, 'man'.

Manu is Noah and Adam rolled into one. According to the Shataphatha Brahmana (1.8.1), he had done a kindness to a fish who, in return, warned him about an impending flood. He built a boat and tied it to the horn of the fish, which towed the boat onto dry land. From this mountaintop, Manu performed the first sacrifice by pouring oblations into the waters—out of which emerged a woman, with whom he fathered a new human race. The Sanskrit for 'human' is *manava*, 'of Manu'—'of the mind', similar to *Homo Sapiens*. Whereas the biblical, Greek, and Mesopotamian floods arose out of divine anger, the Vedic flood was a predetermined, cyclical event.

According to the *Manava Dharmashastra*, Chapter 1, the great sages reverentially approached Manu and bid him reveal the sacred law of the castes, which he had learnt from Brahma, and in turn taught to Bhrigu, one of the ten great sages. The rest of the text then consists of Bhrigu's recitation. This frame of divine authorship added to the appeal and authority of the work, making it seem on par with the Vedas.

The work consists of almost 2700 shlokas consisting of two unrhymed but rhythmic lines of 16 syllables each. The shloka derives from the Vedic anustubh. In the Rig Veda, the anustubh is less frequent than the trisubh or gayatri; but in Classical Sanskrit, the shloka becomes the most common verse form, favoured, among others, by the Itihasas and Puranas.

If the work does have a narrative thread, it is a thin one, and around a third to a half of the material is reduplicated in the *Mahabharata*—although it is not known which is the source and which the borrower. The first chapter deals with origins: of the work, of the world, and of the castes. It is mirrored by the final chapter, on karma, samsara, and moksha. Between these two grand narratives are ten much more mundane chapters on social and religious organization.

In the first chapter, Bhrigu himself outlines the work:

> In this teaching, Manu has declared the origin of the universe and the rules for the transformative rituals, the carrying out of vows and attendance upon (a teacher) and the ultimate rule for the graduation bath; the taking of a wife and the mark of (different kinds of) marriages, the regulations for the great sacrifices and the obligatory rule of the ceremonies for the dead; the mark of the (various) means of livelihood, the vows of a Vedic graduate, what is and is not to be eaten, purification and the cleansing of things; the application of the duties of women, the rules for the generation of inner heat, Freedom, and renunciation, all the duties of a king, and decision-making in lawsuits; the rules for questioning witnesses; the duties of husband and wife; the division of inheritances, gambling and 'cleaning out of thorns'; attendance by commoners and servants, and the origin of confused classes [mixed castes]; the religious duties of (all) classes in extremity, and the rules for restorations [penance]; the threefold course of transmigration that arises from the effects of past actions; the supreme good, and the examination of the virtues and vices of the effects of past actions; the obligatory duties of countries, castes, and families; and the duties of sects of heretics. Learn this teaching, all of you, from me today, just as Manu told it to me long ago when I asked him.

There are over a thousand shlokas pertaining to Brahmanas and nearly as many pertaining to Kshatriyas, suggesting that one of the work's aims is to reassert the relationship between these two varnas. Brahmanas are highly favoured, with, for example, milder punishments for committing the same crime, and, conversely, more severe punishments for those who commit the crime against a Brahmana. Thus, for shouting abuse at a Brahmana, a Kshatriya ought to be fined 100 panas, a Vaishya ought to be fined 150 or 200 panas, and a Shudra ought to be beaten or hanged. But for the same crimes in reverse, the tariffs are, respectively, 50, 25, and 12 panas [8.267].

Women, who are 'without virile strength and Vedic verses' [9.18], must at all times be checked:

> A girl, a young woman, or even an old woman should not do anything independently, even within her home. In childhood a woman should be under her father's control, in youth under her husband's, and when her husband is dead, under her sons'. She should not have independence.
>
> ...
>
> A virtuous wife should constantly serve her husband like a god, even if he behaves badly, freely indulges his lust, and is devoid of any good qualities [5.147-148 & 154].

Still, the men cannot go too far in this, and must watch to the welfare of their women:

> The deities delight in places where women are revered, but where they are not all rites are fruitless. Where the women of the family are miserable, the family is soon destroyed, but it always thrives when the women are not miserable [3.56-57].

That women should be both servile and revered is one of the work's many inconsistencies, or, to be generous, one of its many subtleties. In an article [*An Adi-Dravida's Difficulties*], Gandhi himself remarked that there are 'so many contradictions in the printed volume that, if you accept one part, you are bound to reject those parts that are wholly inconsistent with it.'

In Chapter 2, it is said that 'the father is more important than a hundred teachers, but the mother more than a thousand fathers', and in the next breath that 'between the one who gives him birth and the one who gives him the Veda, the one who gives the Veda is the more important father' [2.145-146].

In Chapter 9, it is said that a woman can procreate with her husband's brother 'in extremity', and in the next breath that this practice is forbidden [9.56-68].

In such blatant cases of contradiction, it may be that the author is following a tradition in Indian logic of first presenting an antithetical view [*purva paksha*, or straw man] to make his own view seem all-the-more persuasive.

Many of the work's inconsistencies arise from a pressing need to reconcile Vedism and Hinduism by squaring the sacrifice with non-violence and vegetarianism. To maintain their power and position, Brahmanas now needed to be pure, as well as knowledgeable or skilled in the sacrifice. Thus, we read that 'killing in a sacrifice in not killing' [5.39]—a contradiction so compressed as to constitute an oxymoron.

Throughout the work, the four varnas are built up, before being torn down in the closing verses:

> Whoever thus sees the self through the self in all living beings achieves equanimity towards all of them and reaches the supreme condition, ultimate reality [12.125].

This emphasis on the varnas, however, is not in the Vedas—born, perhaps, out of a desire or desperation to shore up the Brahmanical position in the face of the threats posed by the Upanishadic and *shramana* movements.

Sometimes, there is a get-out clause for those who kept on reading. For example, a student who has violated his guru's marriage-bed should 'sleep on a heated iron bed or embrace a red-hot metal cylinder and by his death be cleaned'. Or he should 'cut off his penis and testicles, hold them in his two cupped hands, and set out toward the southwest region of Ruin, walking straight ahead until he dies'. But if I were him, I would go with the last option, to 'restrain his sensory powers and carry out the 'Moon-course' vow for three months, eating food fit for an oblation or barley-broth' [11.104-107]. The first two punishments are so severe as to be comical, suggesting that they are purely rhetorical, serving merely to highlight the gravity of the offence.

Carrying on with the comical, there is often leniency for extreme situations. Thus, a Vedic graduate should never emit excrement or urine while facing the wind or looking at fire, a priest, the sun, water, or cows. During the day, he should discharge his urine and excrement while facing north, at night while facing south, and at the two twilights as during the day. But in the shade or in the dark, or when fearing for his life, 'he may do it facing any way he likes, no matter whether it is day or night' [4.48-51].

In London's St Paul's Cathedral, the polyglot Sir William Jones (Chapter 4) is commemorated in stone, holding a copy of the *Manava Dharmashastra*, which, in 1794, he translated into English. Thus, *Manu* was one of the first Sanskrit works to be translated into any European language.

Intoxicated by the sense of Brahmanical superiority, and the treatment of outcasts, Nietzsche, in the *Twilight of Idols* (1889), raves about *Manu*:

> One breathes a sigh of relief at leaving the Christian atmosphere of disease and dungeons for this healthier, higher, and wider world. How wretched is the New Testament compared to *Manu*, how foul it smells!

In India, on the other hand, the *Manava Dharmashastra* has come to be reviled as the principal source for the caste system. In 1927, the political leader and Dalit BR Ambedkar burnt a copy in a gesture that is still widely imitated.

Manu contains all the same moral injunctions as the Bible. But it is, without a doubt, dharma gone too far.

In Rig Vedic times, there were just two varnas, the Arya and the people they overran, the Dasas. In time, 'dasa' came to signify 'servant' or 'slave', and the Dasas came to be known as the Shudras. There was, at least among the Arya, considerable social mobility: for example, a Rig Vedic hymn makes it seem perfectly possible for a physician to marry a miller, and for their son to be a poet (Chapter 2).

However, the Rig Veda also contains the seed of the four varnas, in the *Purusha Sukta*, or Hymn of the Cosmic Man [10.90], according to which the gods created the universe by sacrificing a cosmic man: his mouth became the Brahmin, his arms the Warrior, his thighs the People, and his feet the Servants. The *Purusha Sukta*, which seems anachronistic, and a little too neat, is now regarded as a later insertion into the Rig Veda.

In the Upanishads, there are several varnal reversals, as when King Pravahana instructs Shvetaketu and his father Uddalaka in the doctrine of the five fires and two paths in the afterlife (Chapter 8). Pravahana tells Uddalaka that, up until then, this knowledge had been reserved to the Kshatriyas [Chandogya Upanishad 5.3.7]. In the Great Forest Upanishad [2.1], the Brahmin Balaki proudly pretends to teach King Ajatashatru (the son of Bimbisara of Magadha), who offers him a thousand cows in return; but when it transpires that Ajatashatru has the superior knowledge of Brahman, Balaki humbly asks to be taught by him.

In the Chandogya Upanishad [4.4], the boy Satyakama Jabala, seeking to become a brahmacharya, asks his mother about his patrilineal heritage. His mother tells him: 'I was very busy serving many people when I was young, and I had you. As this was the situation, I know nothing about your lineage. My name is Jabala, and your name is Satyakama.' Later, Satyakama goes to the sage Haridrumata Gautama and asks to be taken in. When Gautama inquires into his lineage, he says, 'Sir, I do not know what my lineage is. When I asked my mother, she said to me: 'I was very busy serving many people when I was young, and I had you. As this was the situation, I know nothing about your lineage. My name is Jabala, and your name is Satyakama.' So, Sir, I am Satyakama Jabala.' An impressed Gautama responds: 'O Somya, go and get me some fuel. I will initiate you, as you have not deviated from truth.'

In the Great Forest Upanishad [3.7.1], Uddalaka cautions Yajnavalkya that if he claims to know what he does not know, taking 'the cows that belong only to the knowers of Brahman', his head will surely fall off.

The veridical mark of a Brahmana, these stories suggest, is not birth, but truth and knowledge.

The original intent of the varnas may have been to create an ideal society. Plato resorts to a similar scheme in conjuring his ideal Republic, with a three-tiered social order consisting of guardians, auxiliaries, and producers, supported by an unknown number of non-citizen slaves. In the *Bhagavad Gita* [4.13], Krishna says: 'The four orders of men arose from me, in justice to their natures and their works.' Later [18.41-47], in discussing the three *gunas*, he tells Arjuna that 'the works of Brahmins, Kshatriyas, Vaishyas, and Shudras are different, in harmony with the three powers of their born nature ... They all attain perfection when they find joy in their work ... Greater is thine own work, even if this be humble, than the work of another, even if this be great.' For Krishna, what determines one's work, and therefore one's dharma, is not one's birth, but one's nature or quality.

After *Manu*, the varnas became more rigid and hierarchical, with the notion of function replaced with that of caste. Beneath the Brahmanas (priests), Kshatriyas (rulers, administrators, warriors), Vaishyas (farmers, herders, artisans, merchants), and Shudras (labouring classes) were the outcastes, that is, the Untouchables and tribal peoples. Arya Kshatriyas and Vaishyas could study the Vedas and take part in sacrifices because, like the Brahmanas, they were *dvija*, or twice-born—the second, spiritual birth being a boyhood initiation into ritual status. Still today, those who have been through this *Upanayana* ceremony are entitled to wear a sacred thread over the left shoulder.

In the Vedas, including the Upanishads, there is no concept of *dvija* or untouchability. In contrast, in *Manu*, the Shudras are required to serve the *dvijas*, while Untouchables ought also to be unseeable, living beyond the village precinct and taking their leftover food in broken dishes. The earliest descriptions of Untouchables are in Fa'hsien (d. 422 CE), the Chinese monk who travelled to India in search of Buddhist manuscripts:

> Throughout the land the people kill no living thing nor drink wine, nor do they eat garlic or onions, with the exception of Chandalas only. The Chandalas are named 'evil men' and dwell apart from others; if they enter a town or market, they sound a piece of wood in order to separate themselves; then men, knowing who they are, avoid coming in contact with them. In this country they do not keep swine nor fowls and do not deal in cattle; they have no shambles or wineshops in their marketplaces. In selling, they use cowrie shells. The Chandalas only hunt and sell flesh [16.3-5].

More than two hundred years later, another visiting monk, Hsuan Tsang (d. 664), outlined the activities of the Brahmanas, Kshatriyas, Vaishyas, and Shudras. That he describes the Shudras as the agricultural class suggests that agriculture has, in the interval, suffered a demotion.

> In these four classes purity or impurity of caste assigns to every one his place. When they marry they rise or fall according to their new relationship ... Besides these four classes, there are other classes of many kinds that intermarry according to their several callings. It would be difficult to speak of these in detail [2.11].

Hsuan Tsang, it seems, has put his finger on the *jatis* ['births'], which is what people mostly have in mind when they speak of the caste system. Arriving in India, Portuguese colonists referred to the varnas and jatis as *casta*, from the Latin *castus*, 'chaste', or, in this instance, 'pure'. Whereas there are only four or five varnas, there are thousands of jatis, typically based on occupation, locality, or tribe. Just as English surnames, such as Baker, Cooper, and Pilcher, often relate to occupation, so Indian ones, such as Acharya [Priest or Teacher], Gandhi [Perfume seller], and Joshi [Astrologer], often relate to jati.

The notion of hereditary trades is hardly unique to India: by the age of about 13, when he lost both of his parents, Aristotle had already received some medical training, because expected to follow in his father's footsteps. In a time when few people grew old, the guild or jati provided training, continuity, identity, security, and status.

But in India the caste system, underpinned by dharma, karma, and samsara, is a lot more developed—and the jatis, though more fluid than the varnas, continue to regulate occupation, marriage, meal-sharing, and more. Most marriages, especially in rural communities, remain endogamous, with mate selection also restricted by language or dialect and dietary habits. Although associated with Hindus, the caste system extends, in various degrees, to Muslims, Christians, and other non-Hindus, and to neighbouring countries such as Pakistan, Bangladesh, Nepal, Bhutan, and Sri Lanka.

Under the Mughals, the caste system may have been as much of a Brahmanical fantasy as a social reality, and it is telling that the word 'caste' is not even an Indian one. Under the Raj, the British reified and rigidified the caste system by, among others:

- Assimilating what they found, read, or heard (often from Brahmanas) to the British class system.
- Shoehorning every jati into a varna to create a false or overstated hierarchy.
- Forcing, by their periodic census, the entire population to make a self-conscious choice of religion and caste, when they may not previously have identified, or strongly identified, with them.
- For a long time before reversing gear, granting administrative jobs and senior appointments only to members of the higher castes; and, last but not least,
- Elevating and canonizing divisive texts such as *Manu*.

Moved by their plight, Gandhi renamed the Untouchables Harijans ['Children of God']. Later, they renamed themselves Dalits [Marathi: Oppressed, Crushed]. In 1956, in Nagpur, BR Ambedkar, himself a Dalit, led a mass conversion of hundreds of thousands to his Marxist reinterpretation of Buddhism, referred to as Navayana Buddhism—leading, at least nominally, to a revival of Buddhism in India.

Ambedkar chaired the committee that drafted the Indian Constitution, which prohibits discrimination on any grounds, including race, gender, religion, caste, and place of birth, and makes special provisions for the advancement of so-called Scheduled Castes and Scheduled Tribes, which, together, account for around a quarter of India's population.

But it is taking time to undo two thousand years of dharma gone awry. People are so warped that they will bend anything, even goodness.

17

THE ARTHASHASTRA OF KAUTILYA

After dharma, artha is the second of the *purusharthas*. The key text on artha is the *Arthashastra* of Kautilya.

Although known from other works, including the *Indica*, the *Arthashastra* had been lost for several centuries.

According to lore, in 1905, a Tamil Brahmin from Tanjore presented a Sanskrit manuscript, written on palm leaves in the South Indian Grantha script, to the newly opened Mysore Oriental Library.

Whatever the case, the librarian and Sanskrit scholar Dr Rudrapatna Shamasastry identified the manuscript as the long-lost *Arthashastra*, and, over the next few years, transcribed it into Devanagari and translated it into English.

The *Arthashastra* is a lengthy but pithy treatise on politics, economics, social organization, foreign relations, and military strategy, intended as a training manual for the king or crown prince—Mauryan or otherwise. Its title has been variously translated as *The Science of Material Gain*, *The Science of Polity*, *The Science of Politics*...

But artha, especially in the Vedas, also applies to the sphere of the individual, or private citizen, in which it means something like prosperity, livelihood, or standing, with connotations of function, purpose, and goal.

In Book 15, on its methodology, the *Arthashastra* defines 'artha' as 'the science by which territory is acquired and maintained—the science of wealth and welfare' [15.1.1-2].

At the end of the same Book 15, it tells us:

> This treatise has been composed by one who, resenting the misrule of the Nandas, rescued this neglected science and used it as a weapon to destroy them and save the kingdom. By following [the principles in] this treatise one can not only create and preserve dharma, artha, and kama but also destroy unrighteousness, material loss, and hatred. It is a guide not only for the acquisition of this world but also of the next [15.1.73, 72, 71].

It is a fascinating work, not only on its own terms, but also for what it tells us about the Mauryan Empire, which, under Ashoka, extended over an area comparable to that of the Roman Empire under Hadrian or Marcus Aurelius. It paints a picture of a highly centralized bureaucracy with elements of a welfare state, more comparable to modern China than to Britain or America.

At its centre is the king, whose first duty is to cultivate self-control: 'A king who has no self-control and gives himself up to excessive indulgence in pleasures will soon perish, even if he is the ruler of the four corners of the world' [1.6.4].

A king is likely to have many enemies, but his greatest enemy is always himself.

In a chapter entitled, *The Superintendent of Cows*, we read that cows are to be belled to better locate them and scare off snakes and tigers. Whoever recovers a stolen cow is entitled to a reward, the full reward if the cow is local and half the reward if it is foreign. Cowherds are mandated: to report missing or unproductive cows, or be held liable for the loss; to provide veterinary care even to aged and infirm cows; and, when a cow dies, to surrender its skin with its brand mark.

Gambling can only take place in authorised gambling halls, where fairness can be enforced, and winnings taxed, at five per cent. Most prostitution is carried out in state-owned brothels, although prostitutes can also set up as sole traders, in which case they are to be taxed a sixth of their income.

Were these directives ever enforced, or even implemented, or is the *Arthashastra*, like Plato's *Republic*, simply promulgating an ideal? That the work is attributed to Kautilya, the enterprising mentor and prime minister of Chandragupta, suggests that it may be something more than pie in the sky.

The text itself alludes to three authors: Kautilya, Chanakya, and Vishnugupta. The consensus is that all three names refer to the man who helped Chandragupta overthrow Dhana Nanda and, for the first time, unite the Indus Valley and Ganges Basin under a single administration—feats made possible by the great learning on display in the work. Vishnugupta, it is suggested, was his personal name, 'Chanak' his father's name, and 'Kautilya' his *gotra* or lineage.

Granting that Kautilya did write the book, stylistic differences suggest a degree of borrowing. The author acknowledges his indebtedness to earlier works, and often juxtaposes earlier authorities and schools of thought. These earlier arthashastras, referred to also in the *Mahabharata*, have all been lost, in no small part because superseded by the work of Kautilya.

The *Mahabharata* also mentions the original work in this genre, called *Dandaniti*, handed down by Brahma at the time of creation. *Danda* refers to the king's rod, so that *Dandaniti* might be translated as *The Science of Law Enforcement*. Danda includes every coercive power of the state: laws, fines, punishments, even the military. It is supported by the treasury, or *kosa*, so that *kosadanda* becomes shorthand for the full might of the state.

According to Kautilya, dharma and prosperity arise from three fields of knowledge: *Dandaniti*, *Varta* [the science of economics], and the Vedas, enlightened by a fourth: *Anvikshaki* [the science of reasoning]: 'Philosophy is the lamp that illuminates all science; it provides the techniques for all action; and it is the pillar which supports dharma' [1.2.12].

'Kautilya', as well as being a gotra, is a wordplay on *kutila*, which means 'crooked' or 'bent'. Certainly, the realpolitik on display, and the degree of practical detail, makes it unlikely that the work was the output of some detached Brahmana.

Indeed, Kautilya is often compared to Machiavelli, though he preceded the Florentine by nearly two millennia (Figure 22). In a lecture entitled, *Politics as a Vocation*, the sociologist Max Weber (d. 1920) opined that, compared to the *Arthashastra*, 'Machiavelli's *Principe* is harmless.'

Kautilya advises a king to cultivate a reputation for foresight by predicting that someone will die and then having him killed. Or to dispose of an enemy, and his cause, by having a statue of a god fall upon him. Or to acquire an air of divinity by going out, in full view of the people, with friends disguised as gods.

This cynical abuse of religion, and Kautilya's overall outlook, seem remarkably modern, and far removed from the more or less contemporaneous Upanishads—but have antecedents in the skepticism and materialism of the Charvakas (Chapter 13).

Figure 22. Fanciful portrait of Kautilya by unknown artist.

As in Machiavelli, the end justifies the means. Both Kautilya and Machiavelli have the prosperity and stability of the state for their end, but, whereas Machiavelli pretends to be for the prince, Kautilya is much more open about this:

> In the happiness of his subjects lies the king's happiness: in their welfare lies his welfare. He shall not consider as good only that which pleases him but treat as beneficial to him whatever pleases his subjects [1.19.34].

When considering a problem, Kautilya often reviews a range of opinions before providing his own moderate, rational view. For instance, senior officials should be selected on the basis not of heredity or malleability, but of character and past performance.

In war, it is forbidden to harm non-combatants or those who have fallen, surrendered, or turned their backs. Once the war has been won, conquered soldiers and subjects are to be treated humanely: 'The conqueror shall substitute his virtues for the defeated enemy's vices and where the enemy was good, he shall be twice as good...' [13.5.3].

Torture is admissible, but there is a long list of persons not to be tortured, including women, the elderly, minors, the disabled, those in a drunken state, those accused of trifling offences, and those having already confessed.

It is for the most vulnerable, and for animals, that the concern is greatest. Pregnant women are entitled to free ferry rides. After the harvest, mendicants and village servants are permitted to glean the grain on crown lands. Provisions for prisoners include wells, lavatories, and bathrooms; adequate time for sleeping, eating, and exercising; and protections against torture or harassment by prison staff. Prisoners are regularly to be amnestied.

Old and infirm horses and elephants are to be fed from the public purse. The punishment for milking cows twice in seasons in which they should only be milked once is to have a thumb cut off. Forests that are exploited for their produce must be sustainably managed to protect and assist wildlife. The fine for harassing, catching, or killing a predatory animal is the same as that for not trying to rescue someone threatened by such an animal.

By the time Ashoka converted to Buddhism and established his veterinary hospitals, the Mauryas already had a proud history of looking after animals.

At 6000 shlokas, the *Arthashastra* is more than twice as long as the *Manava Dharmashastra*. It is divided into 15 books, with 150 chapters covering a total of 180 topics. Book 2, the longest book, contains 36 chapters; Book 11, just one.

The 15 books are entitled:

1. Concerning Discipline [of the king]
2. The Duties of Government Superintendents
3. Concerning Law [Civil Law]
4. Removal of Thorns [Criminal Law]
5. The Conduct of Courtiers
6. The Source of Sovereign States
7. The End of the Six-fold Policy
8. Vices and Calamities
9. The Work of an Invader
10. Relating to War
11. The Conduct of Corporations
12. Concerning a Powerful Enemy
13. Strategic Means to Capture a Fortress
14. Secret Means
15. Methodology

Spies are a recurring theme. The Mauryan state, established by the paranoid Chandragupta and Kautilya, is heavily reliant on an elaborate network of spies, operating both within and without its borders. The functions of this secret service include: testing the loyalty and integrity of officials, flushing out conspiracies, eliminating troublesome elements, monitoring neighbouring states, and destabilizing hostile states.

There are several classes of spies, including counterspies and double agents. Guises recommended for spies include: a wandering ascetic, a Brahmana widow, a *femme fatale*, a cook or saucier, a barber, an astrologer, a buffoon… Languages are an asset, and it might assist to play blind, deaf, or dumb.

Books 6 to 14 treat of war and foreign policy. Although war is the most important means of acquiring territory, peace is generally to be preferred, because more conducive to the creation and enjoyment of wealth.

Many people came to know of the *Arthashastra* by its Mandala theory, which might be thought of as an extension of the dictum that the enemy of my enemy is my friend.

According to the Mandala theory, or *Rajmandala*, a state's immediate neighbours, in the second circle [Sanskrit: *mandala*], are natural enemies, while their neighbours, in the third circle, being their enemies, are natural friends. States in the fourth circle, being the enemies of the friends in the third circle, are, again, natural enemies, and so on. 'The third and fifth states from a [middle] king are states friendly to him; while the second, the fourth, and the sixth are unfriendly' [7.18.1].

Today, New Delhi's diplomatic enclave is called Chanakyapuri ['City of Chanakya'] in honour of Kautilya.

The dark and charismatic Chanakya, having inspired a ream of management and self-help literature, has become a popular figure in India.

18

THE KAMA SUTRA OF VATSYAYANA

In the West, the *Kama Sutra* is known as a book on contortionist sexual positions, or even, erroneously, as a manual for tantric sex.

But it is, in fact, much broader in scope, being the principal, and earliest, extant text on the third of the *purusharthas*, kama. And like its counterparts the *Laws of Manu* and *Arthashastra*, it contains many fascinating insights into the lives and minds of those who breathed it.

In Chapter 8, I defined 'kama' as 'pleasure', but the concept is broader than that, and more nuanced, with connotations of desire, emotional attraction, sensuality, aesthetic appreciation, and *savoir vivre*. The *Kama Sutra* itself defines 'kama' as 'the enjoyment of appropriate objects by the five senses ... assisted by the mind together with the soul' [1.2.11].

> The ingredient in this is a peculiar contact between the organ of sense and its object, and the consciousness of pleasure which arises from that contact is called Kama.

If kama is mind-sense enjoyment, it is in lovemaking that it finds its paroxysm, a state so heightened and divine as to be the source of life and creation:

> In the beginning there was desire, the first seed of mind; sages having meditated in their hearts have discovered by their wisdom the connexion of the existent with the non-existent.
>
> — HYMN OF CREATION, RIG VEDA 10.129

Already in the Rig Veda, desire is the germ of spirit. By the time of the Atharvaveda (1200-900 BCE), Kama has become a god, mentioned in the same breath as Indra, Agni, and Varuna. Atharvaveda Hymn 9.2 is entitled, 'A glorification of Kama as god of desire of all that is good.'

In the Great Forest Upanishad (c. 600 BCE or earlier), King Pravahana tells Uddalaka:

> A fire—that is what a woman is, Gautama. Her firewood is the vulva, her smoke is the pubic hair, her flame is the vagina, when one penetrates her, that is her embers, and her sparks are the climax. In that very fire the gods offer semen, and from that offering springs a man [6.2.13, trans. P. Olivelle].

In one of the earliest passages on karma, quoted in Chapter 8, Yajnavalkya says that man is desire, and becomes as is his desire: 'as is his desire, so is his will; as is his will, so is his deed; and whatever deed he does, that he will reap' [4.4.5].

Like Eros and Cupid, Kamadeva came to be portrayed as flying about shooting arrows of desire. His mount is a parrot, his bow is made of sugarcane, and his arrows are tipped with one of five flowers, each one symbolizing a form of desire.

With the world threatened by the demon Taraka, invincible to all but a son of Shiva, Parvati and the other gods sent Kama, as a last resort, to draw Shiva out of his meditation.

But when Kama fired his arrow, Shiva opened his third eye and burnt him to cinders, leaving the world barren and infertile.

Having been pierced by the arrow, Shiva married Parvati. He later reconstituted Kama, but only as a mental image—which is how true love came to be of the mind.

Holi, the festival of colours, love, and spring, celebrates, among others, the return of Kama into the world.

From the outset, the *Kama Sutra* acknowledges its Vedic heritage, naming Shvetaketu, the son of Uddalaka, as the first human author of a *kamashastra*. Our little Shvetaketu, it seems, has grown up.

Kama is a capacity or art, and, like every art or capacity, requires cultivation: 'Making love without theory is like being an illiterate priest, with no knowledge of grammar, who still pours the offerings into the sacred fire' [1.3.7].

Since life is short, every opportunity is to be seized upon: 'A pigeon to eat is better than a peacock in the sky' [1.2.5 & 23]. The Sanskrit for 'masturbation', I learnt, is *simhakranta*, 'to seize the lion.' Desire is not dirty, pleasure not shameful—so long as the intention is pure.

Inevitably, the wiser we become, the more pleasure we take, and are able to take, even if we would rather call it something else, like tranquillity or joy.

Kama-inspired motifs are common on mediaeval Hindu temples, such as the Kandariya Mahadeva temple at Khajuraho (Figures 23 & 24), suggesting that the prudishness of modern Indians, or, at least, middle class Indians, is born out of Islamic and British sensitivities. According to lore, erotic carvings protected temples from lightning—but not, unfortunately, from the depredations of puritans, and it is on account of their remoteness that those at Khajuraho have survived.

Because the debates on Atma have no practical bearing, the outlook on desire is probably the most important point of difference with Buddhism. According to the *Kama Sutra*, the man accomplished in dharma, artha, and kama 'effortlessly attains the maximum of bliss in this world and the next' [1.2.39].

Kama is the flowering of dharma and artha, but should they ever conflict, or appear to, there can be no doubt that 'dharma is better than artha, and artha is better than kama' [1.2.14].

As for the fourth *purushartha*, moksha, it is mentioned only twice, and one of those times in the context of getting rid of an unwanted lover...

The *Kama Sutra* is attributed to one Vatsyayana, but may in fact be a compendium of older texts.

In the colophon, Vatsyayana tells us that he composed the *Kama Sutra* while a *brahmacharya* in Benares [Varanasi], after pondering the kama shastras of ancient authors.

He often cites these authorities, occasionally adding his own opinion or corrective:

Figures 23 & 24. Erotic carvings on the Kandariya Mahadeva [Great God of the Cave] temple at Khajuraho, Madhya Pradesh, the one-time capital of the Chandela dynasty. Built in the early years of the eleventh century, the temple is the largest and most ornate in the complex.

> The ancient authors consider that since women are incapable of understanding the sciences, it is useless to teach them such things. Vatsyayana notes that they can understand practical science and that practice depends entirely on theory [1.3.3-4].

Other than this, little is known of Vatsyayana. Textual clues suggest that he lived in the second half of the third century CE, possibly in Pataliputra. But owing to the nature of the work, the practices he describes, even if still contemporary, are likely to be several centuries older.

In Chapter 1 of the *Kama Sutra*, Vatsyayana attributes the first formulation of the *Kama Shastra*, in no less than a thousand chapters, to the anthropomorphic bull Nandi ['Joy'], who, as the Doorkeeper of Kailash, overheard the lovemaking of Shiva and Parvati. In another age, Shvetaketu summarized Nandi's *Kama Shastra* in five hundred chapters, which the sons of Babhru condensed into 150 chapters. This being still too long, the work of the Babhravyas [sons of Babhru] came to be divided between several authors, so that the original concept was nearly lost. Thus, Vatsyayana resolved to return to the text of the Babhravyas and summarize it.

Given the nature of the task, Vatsyayana opted for the condensed sutra form, consisting of terse aphorisms intended to be unfolded by a teacher or commentary. The most famous commentary on the *Kama Sutra* is the twelfth or thirteenth century *Jayamangala* of Yashodhara.

Vatsyayana's *Kama Sutra* became the pivotal text on eroticism, cited, among others, by Kokkoka in the *Ratirahasya* (c. 13th century) and Kalyanamalla in the *Anangaranga* (c. 16th century).

The *Kama Sutra* consists of 36 chapters organized into seven parts or books:

1. General Remarks
2. Amorous Advances
3. Acquiring a Wife
4. Duties and Privileges of the Wife
5. Other Men's Wives
6. About Courtesans
7. Occult Practices

Parts 2 and 6 are the longest; the shortest are Parts 4 and 7, with only two chapters each.

The first book describes the lifestyle, routine, engagements, accomplishments, and behaviour of the *nagaraka*, or 'well-bred townsman', to whom most of the text appears to be addressed.

> [The *nagaraka*] must bathe every day, have a massage every two days, soap himself every three days. Every four days, he must trim his beard and moustache, on the fifth or tenth day shave his pubic hair and armpits and, always, scent himself to disguise the smell of sweat from the armpits and be pleasant to contact [1.4.6].

Book 2 is a lot more technical, and famous for it. It begins by classifying men and women into animal types, according to size, endurance, and temperament:

> According to the size of his sexual organ, a man is called a hare, bull, or stallion. The woman, according to type, is called doe, mare, and cow-elephant. Those that are matched form three balanced pairs [2.1.1-2].

This is followed by chapters on embraces, caresses, scratching, biting, oral sex, and more. To master the more acrobatic sexual positions, water immersion is recommended: 'Many amusing positions can be practiced in this way, since they are easier' [2.6.34]. Male and female homosexuality are discussed in terms of a third gender. Other variant practices include role inversion, transvestism, sadomasochism, and group sex.

Book 3 is about how to obtain, treat, and cajole a virgin bride. There is very little discussion of caste. It is said only that 'one should play, marry, associate with one's equals, people of one's own circle' [3.1.20]. Wealth, which is by far the more important consideration, should be evenly matched, because 'whoever marries someone richer becomes inferior in the home' [1.3.24].

The behaviour of the wife, detailed in Book 4, is complicated by the politics of the harem, and her position within it. For the only wife, things are a lot simpler: 'The only wife is totally trusting, considering her husband like a god and completely devoted to him' [4.1.1]. On the bright side, widows can remarry, and there is no mention of *sati*. The text lays out the advantages of having just one wife.

Book 5 discusses sex with other men's wives, which, in general, is not to be recommended. Still, there is an entire chapter on the task of the go-between.

Book 6 addresses courtesans: which men to go for, how to get them, how to behave with them, how to squeeze them for money, and how to get rid of them if they no longer have any.

If all else fails, the final book sets out magical and medicinal formulas for manipulating recalcitrant lovers and enhancing sexual prowess.

Those with a rosy retrospection of free speech should know that it is not until 1962 that the *Kama Sutra* could be published in the UK and US.

In the UK, prosecutions brought by the chillingly named Society of the Suppression of Vice resulted in several publishers being imprisoned. Books that fell afoul of the Obscene Publications Act 1857 could only be circulated privately among the members of a society. For this reason, the traveller and author Sir Richard Francis Burton (d. 1890) founded the 'Kama Shastra Society of London and Benares' to bring out the first English translation of the *Kama Sutra*—a joint effort that bore the name of Richard Burton. Though heavily sanitized, with, for example, the sexual organs abstractly referred to as *lingam* and *yoni*, it soon became one of the most pirated books in the English language.

Today, pornography is ubiquitous, but in a time when it could hardly be found, it is the chapter on sexual positions that excited the most interest. In the 1990s, the chapter on sexual positions from the 1980 Sinha translation began circulating on the Internet, and to this day, many people think of the *Kama Sutra* as nothing more than a sex manual.

But as Vatsyayana warned, making love without theory is like being an illiterate priest, and who would want to get with that?

19

THE RAMAYANA OF VALMIKI

India has several *Itihasas* [Sanskrit, *iti ha asa*, 'so indeed it was']. Of these epic poems, the greatest, and oldest, are the *Ramayana* and *Mahabharata*. Like their Greek counterparts, the *Iliad* and *Odyssey*, the Indian epics feature superhuman heroes subjected to warfare, wandering, and divine intervention. And like their Greek counterparts, they have been polished over the centuries into perfect stories.

The *Ramayana* ['Rama's Journey'] is the tale of Prince Rama, his marriage to Sita, the fourteen-year exile that began on the day of his coronation, the abduction of Sita by the demon king Ravana, and the battles fought to retrieve her. Rama began as a prince of Ayodhya in the kingdom of Kosala [modern-day Awadh, or Oudh]. Later, in mediaeval times, he came to be identified as an avatar of Vishnu—and Sita as an avatar of Lakshmi, who invariably descends with Vishnu.

The heart of the story is pre-Buddhistic, rooted in folk narrative and orally transmitted by bards before being set down into writing, perhaps in the fifth century BCE. The central story is interspersed with philosophy, ethics, and dharma teachings—

embodied by the likes of Rama (the ideal son and king), Sita (the ideal wife), and Lakshmana (the ideal brother). Rama's struggle against the ten-headed Ravana can be read on several levels, such as good versus evil, culture versus nature, or the Aryans versus the Dasas or Dravidians.

Being older than the *Mahabharata*, the *Ramayana* is known as the *Adi Kavya* [First Poem]. The narrative time is anterior to that of the *Mahabharata*, by an entire *yuga*, or world age. The *Ramayana* is set in Treta Yuga, the second of the four yugas in the current time cycle, whereas the *Mahabharata* is set in Dvapara Yuga, the third yuga. Given that a yuga cycle is 4,320,000 years long, that Dvapara Yuga is 864,000 years long, and that Kali Yuga, the fourth yuga, began in around 3102 BCE, this would all be a very long time ago! However, that Rama is a prince of Ayodhya in the kingdom of Kosala seems to link the story to the Age of the Mahajanapadas (Chapter 2). This being Treta Yuga, the evil is not as great as in the *Mahabharata*: for example, although Ravana abducts Sita, he treats her with respect, whereas Dushasana disrobes Draupadi (Chapter 20).

At around 48,000 lines (24,000 shlokas), the *Ramayana* is four times shorter than the *Mahabharata* (c. 200,000 lines)—but still twice as long as the combined *Iliad* (c. 16000 lines) and *Odyssey* (c. 12000 lines). It is divided into seven books, or *kandas*, arranged in narrative sequence, starting with the birth of Rama.

The first and seventh books are thought to be later insertions, aimed, in part, at aligning or reconciling the *Ramayana* with later developments in Hinduism such as devotionalism and the caste system. This often comes at the cost of diluting the work's main message—as when, in Book 7, Rama, acting completely out of character, kills the ascetic Shambuka for performing *tapasya* [austerities, generation of heat and energy], on account, apparently, of his being a Shudra.

The *Ramayana* is attributed to the *Adi Kavi* [First Poet] Valmiki, who began as the brigand Ratnakara.

One day, Ratnakara robbed and threatened to kill the sage Narada, who asked him whether his wife and children, who he claimed to be supporting, would agree to share in his burden of sin. When they did not, Ratnakara returned, repentant, to Narada, who instructed him to chant the name of 'Rama'. As he could not bring himself to utter 'Rama', Narada suggested that he start with 'Mara' [Death]—and, over time, 'Mara' turned to 'Rama' in his mouth. While Ratnakara meditated in the forest, the ants built their anthill [*valmika*] around him. After some years, he emerged from the anthill as a sage. Ratnakara's chanting of 'Mara-Rama' is a good example of the writing-in of *bhakti*, or Hindu devotionalism, into the *Ramayana*.

One day, Valmiki came across a burbling stream, and said to his disciple, "Look, how clear is this water, like the mind of a good man!" While preparing to bathe, he saw a couple of cranes mating. Suddenly, he heard the firing of an arrow, which felled the male crane, leaving its mate to cry out in anguish. Turning towards the hunter, Valmiki exclaimed:

> You shall find no rest for the long years of Eternity
> For you killed a bird in love and unsuspecting.

Later in the day, Valmiki remarked on the unusual metre of this spontaneous utterance—the first ever shloka—which he reserved for the *Ramayana*.

Today, the *Ramayana* exists in several regional recensions and versions, including Buddhist and Jain retellings, and numerous derivations and television adaptations. Certain translations into the vernacular languages, such as the Tamil by Kambar (d. 1250), the Bengali by Krittibas (d. 1461), and the Awadhi by

Tulsidas (d. 1623), have achieved a literary fame all of their own. Unlike the Greek or Roman, Indian mythology is still alive. Rama is worshipped in every part of India, and from Tibet to the Maldives and Philippines. He is so popular that many Hindus, especially in the North, greet one another with 'Ram Ram'. His triumphant return to Ayodhya is celebrated by Diwali, the festival of lights, and Ayodhya is first among the *Sapta Puri* ['Seven Cities'], the seven holiest sites of pilgrimage for Hindus.

It is claimed that the Mughals destroyed a temple that stood at the *Ram Janmabhoomi*, or birthplace of Rama, to replace it with a mosque. In 1992, Hindu mobs tore down the Babri Masjid (Figure 25), leading to riots and nearly two thousand deaths across the subcontinent. Estimating that the land belonged to the government, the Supreme Court ruled that it be handed to a trust to build a Hindu temple, while also compensating the Muslim community for the loss of the Babri Masjid. Prime Minister Narendra Modi, a Hindu nationalist, prematurely inaugurated the Ram Mandir on 22 January 2024, ahead of a springtime general election. Although India is supposed to be a secular state, Kautilya, maybe, would have approved.

The Ramayana

The ageing King Dasharatha of Ayodhya performed a sacrifice in the hope of obtaining an heir, at a time when the gods felt threatened by the depredations of the demon king Ravana.

Owing to past penances, Ravana had been granted a boon that made him invulnerable to any supernatural being—although not to humans or beasts.

Figure 25. The Babri Masjid, named for Babur, in around 1880.

At the behest of Brahma, who had granted the boon, Vishnu agreed to be born as a son of Dasharatha.

In time, Dasharatha's three queens give birth to four sons: Queen Kausalya to Rama, Queen Kaikeyi to Bharata, and Queen Sumitra to Lakshmana and Shatrughna.

One day, Kaikeyi saved Dasharatha's life by leaping down to secure the wheel of their chariot. In reward, Dasharatha gave her two boons, which she decided to reserve.

Rama grew up into the king's favourite. The sage Vishvamitra took him and Lakshmana under his wing, teaching them the knowledge of celestial weaponry and much else besides.

When they came of age, Vishvamitra led the princes to the bridegroom tournament for Sita, the adopted daughter of the Upanishadic King Janaka of Videha (Chapter 5). Sita had emerged from the earth, borne aloft on a lotus.

None of the many princely suitors could bend Shiva's bow, except for Rama, who not only bent but broke it—thereby winning the hand of Sita.

After the wedding, Dasharatha decided to have Rama crowned. But Kaikeyi's maid Manthara ['Humpbacked'] dripped poison into her ear, making her fear for herself and her son Bharata should Kausalya become queen mother.

Thus, Kaikeyi called in her two boons: that Bharata be crowned, and that Rama be exiled for fourteen years.

Desirous to honour his father's promises, Rama left for the forest, accompanied by Sita and Lakshmana. Seeing them go, Dasharatha died from shock and grief.

During these events, Bharata and Shatrughna had been out of the kingdom. When they returned, Bharat refused to be crowned and rushed out in search of Rama. But even he could not persuade him to return. So he placed Rama's sandals on the throne and pledged to rule in his name.

As the people of Ayodhya kept finding him and begging him to return, Rama moved deeper and deeper into the forest. In time, Rama, Sita, and Lakshmana arrived at an auspicious place called Panchavati ['Five Banyan Trees'], where they decided to build a cottage.

But the surrounding forest was inhabited by shapeshifting demons called *rakshasas*. One day, a hideous *rakshasi* [demoness] called Shurpanakha ['Sharp-clawed'] caught sight of Rama and fell in love with him. Adopting the form of a *belle*, she tried to seduce him, and then Lakshmana, before reverting to type and attacking Sita—for which Lakshmana cut off her nose and ears.

Shurpanakha fled to her brother Khara, who attacked Rama and Lakshmana with 14,000 soldiers—only to be defeated. She then fled to Lanka (often assimilated with modern Sri Lanka), to her eldest brother Ravana, who, hearing of Sita's beauty, and desiring her for himself, vowed vengeance.

Ravana forced the demon Maricha to adopt the form of a golden buck and gambol in the sight of Sita, who begged Rama to hunt down the deer. Sensing a ploy, Rama left Sita in the care of Lakshmana, while he pursued the deer into the forest. At a clearing, he shot the deer, and the dying Maricha, mimicking the voice of Rama, cried out to Lakshmana for help.

Lakshmana knew that Rama would not have cried out, or needed to, but Sita implored and then ordered him to go after Rama—going so far as to question his motives for remaining. Before leaving, Lakshmana drew a protective mantra line around the cottage and warned Sita not to cross it.

With Lakshmana gone, Ravana appeared as an ascetic with begging bowl. Sita assembled a plate of fruit and nuts and held it out to him without crossing the line. But the ascetic, who had settled cross-legged under a tree, asked her to bring the plate to him. As soon as she stepped over the line, she found herself in Ravana's clutch, being flown south to Lanka.

Jatayu, the elderly King of Vultures and friend of Dasharatha, tried to rescue Sita, but Ravana cut off his wings. In their search for Sita, Rama and Lakshmana found the mutilated bird, who told them that Ravana had been heading south. Before leaving, Rama performed funeral rites for Jatayu.

In Lanka, Ravana issued strict orders for Sita to be guarded, but treated with respect. Sita fended off Ravana's advances and marriage proposals, and refused to enter his palace.

On the journey south, Rama and Lakshmana met the monkey king Sugriva and his minister Hanuman. Rama helped Sugriva kill his brother Vali and recapture the *vanara* [monkey] throne. A grateful Sugriva sent out monkey scouts in all four directions.

Hanuman alone made it to Lanka, and, after some searching, located Sita in a heavenly garden. With the guards asleep, he showed her Rama's signet ring and assured her that Rama would come for her. He offered to rescue her himself, but she refused—saying that, to be dharma, it must be Rama.

As he prepared to leave, Hanuman wreaked havoc in Lanka, resulting in his arrest and appearance before Ravana. His tail was set on fire, but he broke his bonds, and, by leaping from roof to roof, burnt down the demon capital—before drenching his tail in the ocean and returning to Rama and Sugriva.

Rama assembled an army of all the allies, and, with the help of the monkeys, built a bridge across to Lanka, where he was joined by Ravana's virtuous brother, Vibhishana.

The so-called Battle of Lanka raged for several days. With Lakshmana mortally wounded, Hanuman flew to the Himalayas to fetch a restorative herb. Not knowing which herb to pick, he brought back the entire mountain. After killing Ravana, Rama installed Vibhishana on the throne of Lanka.

Rama doubted Sita's purity and refused to take her back. Wishing to end her life, Sita walked into a burning pyre. But out of the flames came Agni, bearing Sita aloft and vouching for her chastity.

By now, fourteen years had passed and the exile was over. Rama returned to Ayodhya to great fanfare, inaugurating the period of righteous rule known as *Ram Rajya*.

Figure 26. Battle at Lanka, by Sahib Din (c. 1652). Sahib Din was a miniature painter of the Mewar School of Rajasthani painting, and one of the dominant painters of the era. Though a Muslim, he was employed by Hindus to paint on Hindu themes. His floruit coincided with the reign of the fifth Mughal emperor, Shah Jahan.

This would have been the end of the story, had it not been for the insertion of the seventh book.

But the people continued to question Sita's purity, and Rama banished her to the forest. She took refuge in Valmiki's ashram, where she gave birth to Rama's sons, Kusha and Lava.

Valmiki tutored the twins and taught them to sing the *Ramayana*. Their reputation spread, and Rama summoned them to perform at the palace—where they were revealed as his own.

In remorse, Rama asked Sita to return... if only she could prove her purity before an assembly.

In despair, Sita asked to be returned to her mother, the Earth, which opened up to take her in.

20

THE MAHABHARATA OF VYASA

The *Mahabharata* ['Great History of the Bharatas'] is the tale of the royal rivalry between the Pandavas and their cousins the Kauravas, culminating in an epic war to end all wars. It employs the 'story within a story' structure, with the first frame being the narration of the storyteller Ugrasrava Sauti to an assembly of rishis in the sacred forest of Naimisha.

The Kuru kingdom, also known as the Bharata kingdom, rose into the dominant centre of the middle Vedic period (c. 1200-c. 900 BCE), although the date, and even the occurrence, of the Mahabharata War remain unsettled. In the *Mahabharata*, the capital of the Kuru kingdom is Hastinapura ['City of Elephants'], on the right bank of the Ganges—corresponding to modern-day Hastinapur, around 100km northeast of Delhi.

At 1.8 million words in verse and prose, the *Mahabharata* is around four times as long as the *Ramayana*, and the longest epic poem in the world. It begins with a self-conscious claim to completeness: 'What is found here, may be found elsewhere. What is not found here, will not be found elsewhere.' It even contains an abridgement of the *Ramayana*.

Inevitably, order and structure have suffered a little. As it stands, the work is divided into 18 sections, or *parvas*, with a supplementary biography of Krishna known as the *Harivamsha*. The most famous section is Chapters 25-42 of the sixth, Bhishma, parva, known as the *Bhagavad Gita* (Chapter 21).

The central plot, which amounts to a fifth of the work, was compiled from older material in around the fifth century BCE —and the *Mahabharata* is already cited, to illustrate a point of grammar, in the *Astadhyayi* of Panini [6.2.38].

The remainder of the work consists, among others, of myths, legends, genealogies, histories, and philosophical reflections.

The twelfth and longest section, the *Shanti Parva* [Book of Peace], in which the patriarch Bhishma instructs the newly anointed King Yudhishthira on politics, economics, and social organization, is especially abstract.

The principal theme is dharma, in all its complexity, subtlety, and ambiguity. Moral codes are often brought into conflict, with the heroes forced into making compromising choices—and it is Krishna, of all people, who drives them to 'cast aside virtue'.

But by leading the Pandavas to victory, Krishna is fulfilling his higher mission as an avatar, which is to restore dharma at the dawn of Kali Yuga—and Kurukshetra, 'the Field of the Kurus', the battleground of the Mahabharata War, is also known as Dharmakshetra, 'the Field of Dharma'.

Though so tremendously long and varied, the *Mahabharata* is attributed to a single author named Vyasa, who is himself a character within the story, the natural grandfather of the Pandavas and Kauravas through the custom of *nigoya*, whereby a barren widow or wife could, under certain conditions, procreate by another man.

'Vyasa' means 'arranger' or 'compiler', a name or title that may have been granted to several authors—and thus refer to a composite or long line of sages. If the *Mahabharata* were not achievement enough, 'Vyasa' is also credited with the *Brahma Sutra* and the eighteen major Puranas (Chapter 22), and with compiling the Vedic hymns into the four Vedas. In tribute, he is sometimes called Veda Vyasa ['Splitter of the Vedas'], and regarded as a partial, and immortal, incarnation of Vishnu.

An additional frame might be superimposed on the narration of Ugrasrava Sauti. According to lore, Vyasa dictated the *Mahabharata* to Ganesha, who agreed to write it down on condition that Vyasa never pause in his recitation—which, given the length of the work, would have taken a straight two weeks. Vyasa agreed on the counter condition that Ganesha understand whatever he heard before committing it to writing. When Ganesha's pen failed him in mid-recitation, he snapped off one of his tusks as a replacement so as not to interrupt the transmission—whence his epithet, Ekadanta [One-Tusked'].

The influence of the *Mahabharata* can hardly be overstated. The *Bhagavad Gita* alone is one of the world's richest texts: it has come, in Indian society, to assume something of the place of the Bible, and is often read as both a primer and a finisher on Hindu philosophy. Scenes from the *Mahabharata* are popular in Hindu art, including at Angkor Wat in Cambodia. Children continue to be named after characters such as Arjuna, Bhima, Nakula, Sahadeva, and Vidura (pronounced Arjun, Bheem, Nakul, Sahadev, and Vidur, by schwa, or weak vowel, deletion or, to be more precise, syncopation). The 1988 TV adaptation of the *Mahabharata*, in 94 episodes, attracted 97.8% audience share in India, bringing the country, at every screening, to a virtual standstill. When it aired on the BBC—in the afternoon, with subtitles—it achieved a peak audience of 5 million.

The Mahabharata

King Shantanu of Hastinapur had a son called Devavrat with Ganga, goddess of the Ganges.

Years later, Shantanu fell in love with the beautiful Satyavati. But the girl's father refused to let them marry unless Shantanu promised for the throne to bypass Devavrat in favour of his progeny by Satyavati.

Shantanu regretfully declined, but Devavrat, with his father's happiness at heart, vowed to renounce the throne and forever remain celibate.

Because of this oath, Devavrat came to be known as Bhishma ['Terrible']. In recognition of his sacrifice, Shantanu offered Bhishma the boon of choosing the time of his own death.

Soon, Shantanu and Satyavati had two sons, Chitrangada and Vichitravirya. After the king's death, Bhishma helped Satyavati to raise the boys and manage the affairs of the state.

Chitrangada became a mighty warrior king, but died in battle, leaving the boy Vichitravirya to rule. Vichitravirya married two princesses of Kashi, Ambika and Ambalika, but, after seven years of happiness, died, heirless, from tuberculosis.

Satyavati had begun as the daughter of Dasharaja, a fisherman and ferryman on the Yamuna. As a young, fish-smelling woman, she had met a wandering sage, Parashara, who had given her a son, Vyasa, along with the musky fragrance which, much later, reeled in King Shantanu.

Now that her sons by Shantanu had died childless, Satyavati asked Bhishma to marry one or both of Vichitravirya's widowed queens and perpetuate the Kuru clan. But Bhishma refused to break his oath.

So Satyavati summoned her remaining son, Vyasa, from his meditation to impregnate Ambika and Ambalika, according to the custom of *nigoya*. These children, Dhritarashtra and Pandu, became the fathers of the Kauravas and Pandavas. Vyasa had a third son, Vidura, with the maid of the princesses. Bhishma brought up these three boys as his own.

Dhritarashtra was born blind, because Ambika had shut her eyes at the approach of the unkempt hermit; and Pandu was born pale, because Ambalika had recoiled in fear of his touch. Vidura was born at all because, one day, the princesses had sent their maid in their stead. Dhritarashtra's blindness precluded him from sitting on the throne, which passed to Pandu.

Pandu married the princesses Kunti and Madri. One day, while out hunting, he shot at a pair of mating deer, in fact, a sage and his wife in disguise. With his last breath, the sage cursed Pandu to die, if ever he tried to be intimate with his wives.

Fortunately, as a child, Kunti had received boons to pray to a god for a son. Invoking the mantra, she bore Yudhisthira by Dharma, Bhima by Vayu, and Arjuna by Indra.

She then shared the mantra with Madri, who bore the twins Nakula and Sahadeva by the Ashvins.

Each of the god-born Pandavas had an exceptional quality: virtue for Yudhisthira, strength for Bhima, fighting skills for Arjuna, and beauty for Nakula and Sahadeva.

Pandu ruled well and wisely. With the kingdom in good order, he decided to retire to the forest with Kunti and Madri, leaving his blind brother Dhritarashtra to govern on his behalf.

In the forest, one day, he gave in to temptation with Madri, and died—leaving Madri to commit suicide, and Kunti to return to Hastinapura with the five Pandavas.

During all this time, Dhritarashtra had married Gandhari, a princess of Gandhara [Kandahar], who blindfolded herself so as not to see what her husband could not. Dhritarashtra and Gandhari had had a hundred sons and one daughter, known as the Kauravas. Two stood out more than the rest: the eldest, Duryodhana, and the second eldest, Dushasana.

For their tutelage, Bhishma entrusted the 105 princes first to Kripa and then to Drona. The Pandavas excelled in all they did, and their popularity with the people led the Kauravas to fear that they might one day displace their blind father, or them.

What began as cousinly ribaldry and rivalry turned more and more to animosity and enmity. Under pressure from his courtiers, and the people, Dhritarashtra named Yudhishthira as crown prince. But this only inflamed matters—quite literally—with the murderous Duryodhana arranging for the Pandavas to spend the night in a combustible palace.

Alerted to the plot by their uncle, Vidura, the Pandavas dug an escape tunnel for themselves. When the flames died down, the villagers found the charred remains of a forest woman and her five sons, which the Kauravas took for Kunti and the Pandavas.

The Pandavas fled to Panchala, where they lived in a hut disguised as a Brahmin family.

The king of Panchala held a bridegroom tournament for his fire-born daughter, Draupadi. To be successful, the suitor had to pierce the eye of a spinning fish with one of five arrows, while looking down into a water mirror.

Many princes, including the Kauravas, had given it their all. Some could not string or even pick up the bow. With all the Kshatriyas having failed, someone asked if a Brahmana might try—at which Arjuna, in a single shot, pierced the fish's eye with all five arrows.

Disgruntled at the match, Draupadi's brother, Drishtadyumna, secretly followed the Brahmana and his sister back to the hut—to find that the Brahmana was, in fact, Arjuna. Later, in the Kurukshetra War, Drishtadyumna would serve as *senapati* [commander-in-chief] of the Pandava forces.

Also following was the son of Kunti's brother, who had suspected that such an archer could only be Arjuna. For the first time, the Pandavas met their cousin Krishna, who, in the Kurukshetra War, would serve as Arjuna's charioteer.

Upon approaching the hut, Bhima called out to Kunti, saying that they had won a great prize. Thinking the prize to be alms, which Bhima would devour on his own, Kunti said, "Whatever it is, you must all share it!" Thus, Draupadi ended up marrying all five brothers, and rotating annually between them.

Word spread that the Pandavas were alive, and married to Draupadi. Dhritarashtra invited them back to Hastinapura and gave them a large tract of land for a kingdom. In time, they transformed this unpromising land into a prosperous empire, with Yudhisthira, as emperor of Indraprastha, taking fealty from neighbouring kings.

One day, the Pandavas invited the Kauravas to their shiny new palace. Duryodhana would not step onto a glossy floor, believing it to be a pool of water. After being told of his mistake, he saw a pond and fell in—leading even the servants to laugh.

Reeling with envy and resentment, Duryodhana decided to take revenge by exploiting Yudhisthira's penchant for gambling. He organized a game of dice, with his maternal uncle Shakuni, known as the Grand Master of Dicing, playing on his behalf. Having no more wealth to gamble, Yudhisthira progressively staked, and lost: his servants, his kingdom, his brothers, himself, and Draupadi.

Grabbing hold of her hair, Dushasana dragged the former queen, now a slave, into the hall. On the order of Duryodhana, he began pulling at her sari. Draupadi did all she could to defend herself: saying that she was menstruating and could not appear in public; claiming that Yudhisthira, having lost himself first, did not have the right to stake her; and appealing to Bhishma and the other court elderlies—who had been entranced by Shakuni's sleight of hand.

Finally, Draupadi clasped her palms and prayed to Krishna, who spared her modesty by making her sari infinite in length.

With Bhima and the Pandavas vowing revenge, Dhritarashtra brought the proceedings to an end. He gave their freedom and kingdom back to the Pandavas, who returned to Indraprastha.

Having convinced Dhritarashtra that the Pandavas could not be contained by military might, Duryodhana invited Yudhisthira back for another game of dice—this time, with the condition that the losers depart on a twelve-year exile, followed by one year in hiding. Should they be discovered in this thirteenth year, the cycle would start over. As expected, Yudhisthira lost.

Why, you might ask, did Yudhisthira agree to the second game? Yes, he had a weakness for gambling. But more than that, he is a paradigm of the rule follower, unable, as a Kshatriya, to turn down a challenge, or object when his elders did not, or defy the perceived will of the gods... Slavish rule following is why, when Kunti told the Pandavas to 'share their prize', they took her word literally and Draupadi for their common wife.

During their exile, the Pandavas had many adventures. With war in prospect, Arjuna travelled to the Himalayas in quest of celestial weapons. At the end of the twelfth year, a Brahmana's fire sticks became entangled in a stag's antlers, and the priest asked the Pandavas to pursue the fleeing stag.

Thirsty from the chase, Nakula set out to fetch water. He came upon a crystal lake, but a crane warned him that the water would turn to poison if he could not answer its riddles. Nakula ignored the bird, drank of the water, and fell to the ground.

In search of his twin brother, Sahadeva came upon the lake, saw Nakula dead, and was warned by the crane—only to drink of the water and die in his turn. One by one, Arjuna and Bhima suffered the same fate.

Yudhisthira, however, agreed to humour the crane, which revealed itself as a Yaksha [Nature spirit].

The Yaksha asked Yudhisthira over one hundred philosophical questions, including:

> What, if renounced, makes one agreeable?
> —Pride.
>
> What, if renounced, leads to no regret?
> —Anger.
>
> What is grief?
> —Ignorance.

And my personal favourite:

> Who is truly happy?
> —One who can cook in his own home.

Satisfied with Yudhisthira's replies, the Yaksha offered to restore one of his brothers to life. Yudhisthira chose Nakula, on the grounds that Kunti, unlike Madri, already had a living son. Impressed by Yudhisthira's fine application of dharma, the Yaksha restored all of his brothers to life.

He advised the Pandavas to take up disguise and go to the Matsya kingdom, where their dharma would protect them.

The Yaksha and the stag were, in fact, forms of Yama, or Dharma, who wished to test his son's wisdom ahead of the war to come.

In Matsya, the great warrior Arjuna, disguised as a eunuch by the name of Brihannala, taught singing and dancing to the princess Uttara—skills which he had acquired in heaven on his quest for celestial weapons. Yudhisthira moonlighted as a Brahmin counsel, Bhima as a cook, Nakula as a stable boy, Sahadeva as a cowherd, and Draupadi as a hairdresser.

After a year had passed, the Pandavas came out of disguise. King Virata of Matsya offered Uttara in marriage to Arjuna, but he declined on the grounds that one's pupils are akin to one's children. Instead, Uttara was married to Arjuna's son by Subhadra (the younger sister of Krishna), Abhimanyu.

The wedding brought all the Pandava allies together to map out a strategy. Several peace missions failed, with the Kauravas refusing to grant any of the Pandava's requests, even after they had been whittled down to a mere five villages.

War now became inevitable...

21

THE BHAGAVAD GITA, OR SONG OF GOD

The Pandavas managed to assemble seven *akshauhinis* [brigades], to put up against the eleven of the Kauravas. One akshauhini comprised exactly 21,870 chariots, 21,870 elephants, 65,610 horses, and 109,350 infantry—for a total of 218,700 warriors (excluding non-combatant charioteers). The mind boggles at the logistics of feeding and watering 393,660 elephants, let alone the humans and horses.

These figures are not arbitrary, although one cannot be sure of their significance. Chariots, elephants, horses, and infantry are in a ratio of 1:1:3:5. The digits in their numbers (21,870, 65,610, 109,350, 218,700) add up, in each case, to 18, which is also the total number of akshauhinis. The war itself lasted for 18 days. The *Mahabharata* has 18 sections. The *Bhagavad Gita* has 18 chapters... The digits in the number 18 add up to 9, as do the digits in every multiple of 9: 9, 18, 27, 36, 45, 54, 63, 72, 81, 90, 99 (18, i.e. 9)... In the *Gita*, Krishna refers to the human body as 'the castle of nine gates' [5.13], and, from the outset, Dhritarashtra alludes to Kurukshetra as 'the battlefield of life' [1.1]. Whatever the meaning, 9 is an auspicious number in Hinduism.

Although more closely related to the Pandavas, Krishna also had ties with the Kauravas. Thus, Duryodhana and Arjuna arrived in Dwarka on the same day to ask for Krishna's support. Duryodhana, who arrived first, found Krishna sleeping, and sat waiting at the head of the bed. Arjuna, when he arrived, sat, in reverence, at the foot of the bed. When Krishna awoke, it is Arjuna whom he first saw. Because of this, he offered to help them both, offering them the pick of either himself or his vast army. Arjuna chose Krishna, leaving Duryodhana to believe that he had got the upper hand. On the battlefield, Krishna would serve Arjuna as his charioteer.

Vishnu appears, in avatar form, in both the *Ramayana* and the *Mahabharata*. But unlike Rama, Krishna knows that he is Vishnu, and on the battlefield, reveals himself to Arjuna in his sublime yet terrible universal form. J. Robert Oppenheimer, the 'father of the atomic bomb', had read the *Bhagavad Gita* in the original Sanskrit and been profoundly affected by it—to the point of nicknaming his car Garuda, after the eagle-like *vahana* of Vishnu. He recalled that, upon witnessing the first nuclear detonation on July 16, 1945, he thought of Vishnu in his universal form, and of these verses in particular:

> If the radiance of a thousand suns were to burst at once into the sky, that would be like the splendour of the mighty one ... Now I have become Death, the destroyer of worlds [11.12, 32].

Fittingly, the *Mahabharata* contains the earliest discussion of the 'just war', that is, the morally justifiable war. The Pandava brothers agree to rules of combat, such as protection of non-combatants and fair treatment of captives, that call to mind the much later Geneva Conventions. Still, in the heat of battle, they sometimes break the rules—and none more so than Bhima.

Figure 27. Krishna Vishvarupa. Vishnu's theophany, depicted c. 1740. Smithsonian National Museum of Asian Art, Washington, D.C.

The *Bhagavad Gita* opens on the blind king Dhritarashtra asking his advisor Sanjaya what is happening at Kurukshetra:

> On the field of Truth, on the battlefield of life, what came to pass, Sanjaya, when my sons and their warriors faced those of my brother Pandu?

Sanjaya had received the gift of divine vision from Vyasa, enabling him to see the events from afar in the palms of his hands. The rest of the *Gita* consists of Sanjaya's transmission of the philosophical conversation that took place between Krishna and Arjuna at the beginning of the battle, punctuated by the very occasional narrative interruption. In this conversation, it is, of course, Krishna who does most of the talking.

Chapter 1. As the drums and conch shells are sounding, Arjuna asks Krishna to drive into the midst of the battlefield. From this vantage point, he can see the supreme commander of the Kaurava forces, none other than his beloved Bhishma—who, like his revered teacher Drona, had taken a terrible vow to serve the sitting king of Hastinapura, whomever he might be.

Heartbroken at the thought of killing his cousins, elders, and teachers, Arjuna throws down his great bow Gandiva:

> O, day of darkness! What evil spirit moved our minds when for the sake of an earthly kingdom we came to this field of battle ready to kill our own people?

Chapter 2. In Chapter 1, Arjuna had presented three arguments against fighting, founded in consequentialism, virtue ethics, and deontology. First, why gain a kingdom if those we want it for are all dead? Second, fighting and killing our enemies makes us no better than them. And third, infighting in a family undermines the social order.

Krishna counters these three arguments: death is an illusion; a warrior's duty is to fight; and doing one's duty is the greatest good. The wise despair neither for the living nor for the dead, because life and death pass away, and we have all been, and will all be, for all eternity:

> If any man thinks he slays, and if another thinks he is slain, neither knows the ways of truth. The Eternal in man cannot kill: the Eternal in man cannot die.

In fact, the war is an opportunity for Arjuna to do his duty as a Kshatriya, and there is no greater good or greater happiness than to do one's duty, without worrying about the outcome. We should do our work, not for its reward, but for its own sake, without being moved by apparent success or failure.

> Work done for a reward is much lower than work done in the Yoga of wisdom ... How poor those who work for a reward!

Yoga is tranquillity of mind, without which there cannot be joy. Pleasure leads to desire, and desire to passion, which upsets and confuses the mind. When driven by desire, we forget our duty and forsake the peace that it brings.

> When a man dwells on the pleasures of sense, attraction for them arises in him. From attraction arises desire, the lust of possession, and this leads to passion, to anger. From passion comes confusion of mind, then loss of remembrance, the forgetting of duty. From this loss comes the ruin of reason, and the ruin of reason leads man to destruction ... There is no wisdom for a man without harmony, and without harmony there is no contemplation. Without contemplation there cannot be peace, and without peace can there be joy?

Chapter 3. There are two roads to perfection: Jnana Yoga, the Path of Knowledge, and Karma Yoga, the Path of Action. Not by mere renunciation or refraining from action does one attain freedom from action. Action is unavoidable; so, instead, we should aim at unattached or desireless action.

> Even as the unwise work selfishly in the bondage of selfish works, let the wise man work unselfishly for the good of all the world ... And do thy duty, even if it be humble, rather than another's, even if it be great. To die in one's duty is life: to live in another's is death.

One might here be reminded of Sartre and the existentialists: choice is unavoidable, and not to choose is in itself to make a choice—the choice of death.

Chapter 4. Krishna speaks of himself and his role as an avatar: 'In any way men love me, in that same way they find my love: for many are the paths of men, but they all in the end come to me.'

He returns to selfless action. The true sacrifice is not of butter, but of our own soul. And greater than any sacrifice is wisdom, which is the end, and enabler, of all holy work.

Chapter 5. Which, asks Arjuna, is better, renunciation or holy work? Both are a path to unification with Brahman, but selfless action is better. In any case, the difference is not so great as it seems, since renunciation is hard to attain without selfless action, and selfless action does not feel like work.

Chapter 6. It is through work that the Yogi surrenders his earthly will, climbs the heights of Yoga, and finds peace—and in peace, God. Then, he sees himself in every being, and every being in him: 'And when he sees me in all and he sees all in me, then I never leave him and he never leaves me.'

The greatest Yogi dwells beyond austerity, knowledge, or work, in the love of Krishna. It takes many lives to become a Yogi, but with each new life we begin where we left off.

Past strivings will not be forgotten.

Chapter 7. Krishna discusses himself as the refuge supreme. People know him only as a human representation, and can scarcely imagine his true nature, drowning as they are in the desire-driven delusion of division.

There are several parallels with Plato, as when Krishna describes himself as 'the intelligence of the intelligent' and 'the beauty of the beautiful'. Or when he identifies four kinds of men who are good and who love him: the man of sorrows, the seeker after knowledge, the seeker of something he treasures, and the man of vision. Similarly, in Plato, the souls that rode highest and gazed longest upon the Universals are incarnated as philosophers, musicians [artists], and true lovers. In Plato's *Phaedrus*, Socrates lays out the four forms of divine madness [*theia mania*]: prophecy from Apollo; mysticism from Dionysus; poetry from the Muses; and love, the highest form, from Aphrodite and Eros.

For Plato as for Krishna, it is the (true) lover who is nearest to God and salvation.

If people are too little in their love, it is because they are protecting against non-divine madness, when there are, in fact, other, less limiting, ways to do so.

Chapter 8. When Arjuna asks about Brahman, Atman, and Karma, Krishna defines Brahman as the Eternal, Atman as his Spirit in man, and Karma as the force of creation. He who, out of love, trains his mind on Brahman, and has Brahman ever in his mind, goes to Brahman, and never returns to this world of death and sorrow.

Chapters 9 & 10. Krishna reveals that all things come in and out of him in cycles. Yet, he is greater than his creation. Those who know and love him find their refuge in him. They are free from delusion, and free from all evils. Those who follow the more complicated Vedic path return after a time to the world of death, but those who worship him, and have faith in him, shall come to him and forever be freed from the bonds of Karma. This path to salvation is open to all: sinners, women, Shudras, everyone. Arjuna accepts Krishna as the Supreme Brahman.

Chapter 11. Arjuna asks to see Krishna in his universal form. As this cannot be done with mortal eyes, Krishna gives him divine sight. Even then, the vision is blinding and incomprehensible.

And for all its wonder [Greek, *thauma*], it is also wounding [Greek, *trauma*]:

> I am all-powerful Time which destroys all things, and I have come here to slay these men. Even if thou dost not fight, all the warriors facing thee shall die...

Arjuna begs Krishna to return to his human form. Krishna complies, saying that, until this day, no man or god had ever seen him in his universal form. Only by love might they hope to apprehend it: not by study, or ritual, or sacrifice, or austerity, or alms, but only by love.

Chapter 12. The surest and easiest path to Brahman is surrender in love of the fruit of one's actions.

> The man whose love is the same for his enemies or his friends, whose soul is the same in honour or disgrace... this man is dear to me. But even dearer to me are those who have faith and love, and who have me as their End Supreme.

Chapter 13. Krishna distinguishes the field from the knower of the field. The field is more than just the body, and includes consciousness, mind, and 'psychology'. The knower of the field is everything that tries to rise above the field: humility, sincerity, harmlessness, freedom from attachments, absence of the thought of 'I', solitude, perspective, devotion...

The end of the knower is to go beyond death by recognizing his own Atman, or unbound spirit, and becoming one with it.

Chapters 14 & 15. The three *gunas* [constituents of nature], Sattva, Rajas, and Tamas—light, fire, and darkness—restrain the Knower from the knowledge of Atman.

In any person, one of the gunas may prevail over the other two: Sattva binds to earthly happiness and lower knowledge, Rajas to passion and attached action, and Tamas to ignorance and sleepy dullness.

The man of vision who sees that he is being driven round and round by the powers of nature rises above them, and, in so doing, frees himself from death and sorrow.

Chapter 16. Krishna contrasts the man of heaven to the man of hell. Men of a hellish nature are 'bound by hundreds of vain hopes' and 'beset with innumerable cares'.

> Led astray by many wrong thoughts, entangled in the net of delusion, enchained to the pleasures of their cravings, they fall down into a foul hell ... In their chains of selfishness and arrogance, of violence and anger and lust, these men hate me: they hate me in themselves and in others. In the vast cycles of life and death, I inexorably hurl them down to destruction...

Three are the gates to hell: lust, anger, and greed.

Chapter 17. Devotion has to be sincere, and without ulterior motive. Intention is everything.

> A gift is pure when it is given from the heart to the right person at the right time and at the right place, and when nothing is expected in return. But when it is given expecting something in return... the gift is of Rajas, impure.

Chapter 18. The true renunciate is not one who renounces work, but the reward of work. In all four varnas, people attain perfection when they find joy in their work, however humble or imperfect it might be, when their work is their worship.

The highest work is to teach this secret doctrine to those who are fit to receive it, and to them only. Wisdom is not for those who are lacking in love, or goodwill, or diligence.

Even if people do not understand all that they are told, still, by faith and adoration, they can achieve liberation.

The *Bhagavad Gita* ends, and the *Mahabharata* takes up, when Arjuna picks up his bow to fight.

In revenge for the game of dice, Bhima tore out Dushasana's arms, broke open his chest, and drank his blood, before washing Draupadi's hair in it. Two days later, on the eighteenth day, he killed Duryodhana by breaking the thigh which he had slapped at Draupadi.

When the dust settled, only 18 warriors had survived, eight on the Pandava side (including Krishna and the five Pandavas) and three on the Kaurava side. In particular, the Upapandavas, Draupadi's five sons by each of the Pandavas, had all perished, as had Arjuna's other sons, Abhimanyu and Iravan.

On the fifteenth day, to defeat Drona, Krishna urged Yudhisthira to tell Drona that his son Ashwatthama had died. But Yudhisthira refused to tell a lie. So that Yudhisthira would not have to lie, Krishna suggested that they kill an elephant named Ashwatthama. Because Yudhisthira never lied, Drona believed him when he said that Ashwatthama (the elephant) had died. As Drona bowed down in grief, Drishtadyumna lobbed off his head.

Is a misleading truth morally superior to a lie? Vyasa, or the author of the *Mahabharata*, suggests not when he has Yudhisthira's chariot, which floated on a cushion of moral righteousness, come crashing to the ground.

The Kauravas, as moral parasites, thrived by exploiting the conventional morality of the Pandavas, and could only be brought down, for the greater right, and greater good, by breaking loose from the paradigm.

By fighting out of devotion to Krishna and merging with the godhead, Arjuna abandoned the good for the right, the ethical for the just. Like the Stoic archer, he focused on the procedure rather than the outcome. In the long-term, proceduralism, no matter how difficult, leads to better outcomes, as demonstrated by Gandhi and his *satyagraha* (Chapter 13). Not coincidentally, Gandhi wrote a commentary on the *Gita*. He also translated Plato's *Apology* into Gujarati—while in prison.

From a bed of arrows fired by Arjuna, the dying Bhishma instructed the newly anointed King Yudhisthira on statecraft.

Yudhisthira ruled Hastinapur and Indraprastha for 36 years, before abdicating in favour of Abhimanyu's son, Parikshit.

Around this time, a hunter mistook Krishna for a deer; like Achilles, he died from a poisoned arrow in his one vulnerable part, his heel.

Having dismissed their retinues and cast off their fineries, the Pandavas journeyed to Mount Meru, followed only by a stray dog. One by one, they fell on the ascent, leaving only Yudhisthira with the dog to arrive at the gates of heaven. According to Yudhisthira, Draupadi fell for being partial to Arjuna, Nakula and Sahadeva for their vanity, and Arjuna and Bhima for their pride.

Indra invited Yudhisthira into heaven, but refused to admit the dog. After remonstrating with Indra, Yudhisthira turned away, saying that he could not bring himself to abandon his faithful companion. At this, the dog revealed himself as Yama, who informed his son that this had been his final test and reassured him that his wife and brothers were waiting for him in heaven. The ascent of Yudhisthira marked the beginning of Kali Yuga.

Parikshit ruled for sixty years before dying from a snakebite. He is eulogized in Hymn 127 of the Atharva Veda: 'Happily thrive the people in the land where King Parikshit reigns.' He was succeeded by his son Janamejaya, who, in anger, performed a snake sacrifice to destroy all snakes. It is at this sacrifice that Vyasa's disciple Vaishampayan recited the tale of his ancestors to Arjuna's great grandson—the tale later retold by Sauti.

Some say that it was Parikshit and Janamejaya, rather than Vyasa, who split the Vedas.

For being the literal word of God, the *Gita* is often looked upon as a revealed text, on a par with the *Upanishads*. Certainly, manuscripts of the *Gita* show a lot less variation than the *Mahabharata* as a whole. Like the *Mahabharata*, the *Gita* is attributed to Vyasa, but may have been written as a separate work, and is increasingly treated as such.

Its themes suggest that it is rooted in a time of religious flux, when even great warriors like Arjuna took to questioning the ethics of war. And what it represents is an attempt to resolve the tension between competing strands of Hinduism, including Vedic ritualism (Karma Yoga), Upanishadic wisdom (Jnana Yoga), and shramana asceticism (Raja Yoga), by integrating them into devotionalism (Bhakti Yoga) and bringing this to the fore. This also served to democratize the religion, which, to ordinary people not given to sacrifice, study, or meditation, must have seemed remote and elitist.

After the *Gita*, everyone, including the Vedic householder, Shudras, Dasas, and women, could achieve the moksha of the renunciate through inner renunciation of the fruits of action. Indeed, this is the true meaning of renunciation, rather than the monkish idleness which is of Tamas. Such is the emphasis on liberation that many historical commentators on the *Gita* have regarded it as a *mokshashastra* rather than a *dharmashastra*.

According to temperament, people may be better suited to Karma Yoga, Jnana Yoga, or Raja Yoga, but, in any case, they all lead to surrender, that is, to Bhakti Yoga. Those unable to partake in Karma Yoga, Jnana Yoga, or Raja Yoga might instead go straight to Bhakti Yoga, which is not only simpler but surer —so long as one has the faith, or rather, the love, without which salvation, whatever the route, is impossible.

Thus, in the thousand years from around 1200 to 200 BCE, there has been a shift from the teleological (results-driven) reasoning of ritual sacrifice to the procedural (action-driven) reasoning of devotion, via the deontological (rules-driven) reasoning of dharma and karma—a shift, if you prefer, from utilitarianism to virtue ethics, via deontology.

In criticism, it might be said that if motiveless action leads to peace, joy, dignity, and the best long-term outcomes, then the person who, knowing this, engages in motiveless action is not truly motiveless. Maybe the answer is that the motivelessness need only be in the moment.

Also, by claiming that the soul is eternal and making light of death and murder, is Krishna not, like many a terrorist, using religion to justify atrocity? Gandhi was moved by his reading of the holy book, but then so too was his assassin, the Hindu Nationalist Nathuram Godse, who carried a copy of the *Gita* all the way to the gallows. In the *Mahabharata*, the Kurukshetra War is only fought in the last resort, after a great deal of soul-searching by a virtuous prince, in other words, by an elite. But, surely, not everyone can be relied upon to get this right. Krishna, it seems, has as much faith in us as he asks out of us.

But isn't this the final point of the *Mahabharata*? —that, in the end, nothing is harder than to be moral.

22

THE PURANAS: VISHNU, SHIVA, AND DEVI

The shift from ritual sacrifice and asceticism to devotionalism [*bhakti*] gave rise, from 400 BCE to 300 CE, to three dominant theistic schools: Vaishnavism, Shaivism, and Shaktism, with Shiva, Vishnu, and Devi [Shakti] promoted above the Vedic gods. Their mythologies and traditions are documented, above all, in the Puranas.

The vast and diverse Puranas are classified as remembered texts [*smriti*], as opposed to revealed texts [*shruti*]. They were composed in a prakritized Sanskrit or a local vernacular, in the main, for the edification of women and the humbler *varnas*. Thus, they are more accessible and relatable (if not necessarily more readable) than the Vedas and Upanishads, and their prescriptions rarely require the presence of a Brahmin priest.

'Purana' means 'ancient', and the designation of 'Purana' conferred an air of antiquity and authority upon a partisan tract. Among all the claimants, eighteen Major and eighteen Minor Puranas are recognized—not least because 18 (1 + 8) is an auspicious number in Hinduism (Chapter 21). Between them, the eighteen Major Puranas contain over 400,000 *shlokas*, albeit with considerable overlap in content. They are highly sectarian, extolling the virtues of a particular god such as Vishnu, Shiva, or Devi, without, however, excluding the other gods. Compared to the Mahapuranas, the Upapuranas [Minor Puranas] are shorter and later. There are also other types of Purana, including Sthalapuranas on the history and significance of a particular temple or locality, and Kulapuranas on the cultural heritage of a particular caste or community.

The elevated status of the Mahapuranas derives in part from the naming of Vyasa as their author, the same Vyasa who compiled the Vedas, composed the *Mahabharata* and *Brahma Sutra*, and never ever suffered from writer's block. The Puranas are thought of as later than the epics. However, certain Puranas (it is never clear which) are mentioned in the epics and even in the Vedas, for example, in Hymn 7 of Book 11 of the Atharva Veda. The Chandogya Upanishad names the four Vedas, before adding: 'The Itihasas and Puranas are the fifth Veda' [7.1.4]. Perhaps Vyasa did write a Purana, or Puranic text, which came to be expanded into a genre—with most of the Puranas, or Puranic material, having been written after the Itihasas.

In theory, a Purana is supposed to treat of five subjects, the so-called *panchalakshana*: creation [*sarga*], destruction and secondary recreations [*pratisarga*], genealogies of gods and patriarchs [*vamsa*], creation of the human race [*manvantara*], and genealogies and histories of kings [*vamshanucarita*].

In fact, the *panchalakshana* make up only a small fraction of their encyclopaedic contents, which also include: cosmology, the purusharthas, ritual sacrifices, religious observances and festivals, rites of passage, places of pilgrimage, donations, construction of temples, geography, astronomy, grammar, philosophy, medicine, charms and spells, folk tales, love stories, and much else besides.

Figure 28. An apsara, who would dance for the gods and seduce sages to prevent them from attaining yogic powers. Uttar Pradesh, 12th century. Metropolitan Museum of Art, New York.

Gods and kings are accompanied by a vast cast of mythical beings including asuras [anti-gods], rakshasas [demons or goblins], nagas [serpents], yakshas [nature spirits], gandharvas [celestial musicians], and apsaras [celestial courtesans and dancers] (Figure 28). Stories such as the Pillar of Fire, in which the gods—often Brahma, Vishnu, and Shiva—compete for supremacy, are especially common.

With worship [*puja*] replacing Vedic sacrifice, the Puranas also contain detailed instructions for the construction of devotional icons and statues, or *murtis* ['forms', 'embodiments']. Common aspects of a god include *Raudra* [Fearsome, terrifying] and *Shanta* [Peaceful, benevolent]. Each aspect of a god has its proper number of appendages (arms, heads, eyes...), posture, gestures, colours, proportions, vehicles, weapons and symbols, consort and companions, and rituals for consecration [*prana pratishtha*, 'infusing of breath']. For statues, white marble is predominant in northern India, and dark granite in southern India. Brahma is often represented as emerging from a lotus stemming from the navel of Vishnu in his recumbent (Narayana) aspect. Forms of Shiva have three horizontal ash-white lines across the forehead [*vibhuti*]. Forms of Vishnu have three vertical lines, the two outer ones being white and the central one being red [*nama*]. Gods may also be represented in aniconic forms, such as the *shaligram* [fossilized stone or ammonite] for Vishnu, the *linga* for Shiva, and the *yoni* for Devi. Worshippers can interact with a murti in various ways, among others, by adorning it, offering it gifts, or venerating it. Veneration can take several forms such as singing *bhajans* [devotional songs] or making circular motions with an oil lamp [*arati*]. Specifications for the construction of murtis are also contained in artisan manuals known as Shilpashastras.

The most popular, and also the most Sanskritized and literary, Purana is the *Bhagavata Purana*. According to one of its verses [1.3.40], it is the literary incarnation of Krishna. Like many an Indian text, it takes the form of a 'story within a story', with the frame story being related by Shuka, son of Vyasa, to Parikshit, grandson of Arjuna. Although it treats of a diversity of topics, it is best remembered for Book 10 on the childhood of Krishna, starting with his attempted murder by King Kamsa and fostering by the cowherds Nanda and Yashoda.

Vaishnavism, the veneration of Vishnu and his many avatars, includes sub-sects such as Krishnaism and Ramaism. Vishnu ['All-Pervasive'] famously has a thousand names, including Hari, Narayana, and Vasudeva—pointing to this multifaceted god's syncretic nature.

Among the *Trimurti*, Vishnu is thought of as the preserver, alongside Brahma the creator and Shiva the destroyer. As the restorer of dharma, he has ten primary avatars, known as the *Dashavatara*: fish, turtle, boar, man-lion, dwarf, Rama with an Axe, Rama, Krishna, Buddha, and the yet-to-come Kalki, who will usher in the apocalypse at the end of Kali Yuga. As the fish Matsya, Vishnu saved Manu and the Vedas; as the turtle Kurma, he assisted the Devas and Asuras in churning the Ocean of Milk for *amrita*, the elixir of immortality.

Vishnu's consort, Lakshmi, is the granter of wealth material and spiritual: when he descended as Rama, she came as Sita; when he came as Krishna, she descended as Radha. The love between Radha and Krishna is the material of the *Gita Govinda*, by the thirteenth century poet Jayadeva. Vishnu's *vahana* is the eagle-like Garuda, who lent his form to the state insignia of both Thailand and Indonesia, and his name to Indonesia's flag-carrying airline. In his four hands, he bears a lotus, a conch, a mace, and a demon-slaying discus, the Sudarshana Chakra. In his Narayana aspect, he reclines in a yogic slumber on the serpent Shesha, as they float on the primordial Ocean of Milk: Shesha forms a canopy over him with his seven or thousand hoods, while Brahma emerges out of a lotus stemming from his navel and Lakshmi rubs his feet. In another recumbent posture, he is the baby Krishna, lying supine on a lotus leaf and sucking his toe—thereby signifying that, by his deeds, a Shudra, born of the foot, can become a Brahmana, born of the head. Vaikuntha, Vishnu's heaven on Mount Meru, is a place of golden palaces and hanging gardens.

Shaivism, the veneration of Shiva ['the Auspicious One'], traces its origins to the volatile Vedic god Rudra and perhaps even to the yogin featured on the Indus Valley Pashupati seal. According to the Aitareya Brahmana [3.33], the gods produced Rudra to punish Prajapati for committing incest with his daughter, Ushas. Although only a minor god in the Samhitas, in the Shevtashvatara Upanishad, Rudra, now Rudra-Shiva, emerges as the paramount deity.

Shiva is generally portrayed as the destroyer, who annihilates the universe at the end of each cosmic cycle, and as the ascetic Lord of Yoga. But in death and destruction, there is also life and creation, and his chastity is matched by his virility. His phallic column, or lingam, is commonly seated on a yoni, or spouted dish, and doubles up as an *axis mundi.* When Brahma lied about having overflown it (Chapter 6), Shiva emerged in his fierce Bhairava form and cut off one of Brahma's five heads—which, in retribution for attacking a Brahmana, stuck to his hand. In another story, about the origin of the lingam, Shiva entered a forest to meditate, but the wives of the other ascetics fell madly in love with him. To punish him, the other ascetics severed his genitals and fixed them into the ground. But terrible consequences followed, and the ascetics agreed to give worship to the lingam. The most important day in the Shaivite calendar is Maha Shivaratri ['Great Night of Shiva'], which, among others, marks the apparition of the blazing lingam [*lingabhava*].

As well as an ash-covered yogin, Shiva also appears as Nataraja, the Lord of the Dance (Figure 29), whose rhythms create, sustain, and destroy the universe. Performed with joy, his Tandava is creative; but performed with ire, it is destructive. Parvati responds to Shiva's Tandava with a dance of her own, the Lasya. The Tandava and Lasya in their various forms are incorporated into classical Indian dance.

Figure 29. Shiva Nataraja, Lord of the Dance. Chola bronze, 10th century. There is a 2m metre Nataraja outside the European Organization for Nuclear Research (CERN) in Geneva. Note, among others, the symbol-rich matted hair, the cobra wrapped around the arm held out in the abhaya 'fear not' mudra, the drum (damaru) and flame (Agni) in the rear hands, and the trampling, on the lotus pedestal, of the dwarf of ignorance.

A third aspect of Shiva is the androgynous Ardhanarishvara, split down the midline between Shiva on the right-hand side and Parvati on the left. Vishnu too can be androgynous: adopting the form of the enchantress Mohini, his female avatar, he had a son, Ayappan, with… Shiva—a son who serves as a bridge between Vaishnavism and Shaivism.

In murtis, Shiva may be accompanied by Parvati, their two sons Skanda and Ganesha, and his *vahana* the bull Nandi. One day, Shiva chopped off Ganesha's head for coming between him and Parvati—and placated Parvati by replacing it with that of an elephant. Shiva's marks and symbols include a third eye, matted hair, a crescent moon headdress, a blue throat [*Shiva Nilakanta*], a cobra around the neck, a tiger skin, a trident, a begging bowl, and a rosary for the recitation of mantras. In his fierce Bhairava form, Shiva carries Brahma's skull [*kapala*].

Shiva worship assumes many forms, ranging from the austere and ascetic to the Tantric and deliberately transgressive—the most extreme example of the latter being the extinct Kapalikas [Skull-bearers] who worshipped Shiva in his disinhibited Bhairava form with offerings of alcohol, meat, and bodily fluids. The Kapalikas matted their hair and smeared their naked bodies with ash from cremation grounds. They went about with a skull for a begging bowl—obtained, allegedly, from a human sacrifice. By breaking with convention, the Kapalikas hoped to acquire the powers [*siddhi*] of the gods, who, like them, embraced contraries. In the dissolution and expansiveness of drunkenness, or the abandon and tranquillity of orgasm, they may have seen reflections of the union of the individual with the universal, of Atman in Brahman. Shiva's heavenly abode is Shivaloka on Mount Kailash.

The female energy, or Shakti, of Shiva came to be embodied as Devi or Shakti, reinvigorating the long, pre-Aryan tradition of mother goddess worship in India. 'Devi' or 'Shakti' may also refer to any Hindu goddess, especially the *tridevi* of Parvati, Lakshmi, and Saraswati (Brahma's consort), who are envisioned as aspects of a Universal Goddess.

The Goddess is extolled even in the androcentric Rig Veda, in the *Devi Sukta*:

> I am the queen, the gatherer-up of treasures, most thoughtful, first of those who merit worship... I created all worlds at my will, without any higher being, and permeate and dwell within them. The eternal and infinite consciousness is I, it is my greatness dwelling in everything.
>
> — RIG VEDA 10.125

Some of her other names are Prakriti and Maya, associating her with nature, matter, and illusion.

A section of the *Markandeya Purana* dedicated to the Goddess, the *Devi Mahatmya* ['Glory of the Goddess'], describes her as the supreme power and creator of the universe:

> I resemble in form Brahman,
> from me emanates the world,
> which has the Spirit of Prakriti and Purusha,
> I am empty and not empty,
> I am delight and non-delight,
> I am knowledge and ignorance,
> I am Brahman and not Brahman.
>
> — DEVI MAHATMYA 152

The Goddess has a benevolent and nurturing aspect but also a terrifying and destructive one. She is most often manifested as the warrior goddess Durga ['Impassable', 'Invincible']. Created by the Trimurti and the lesser gods to overcome the buffalo demon Mahishasura, Durga embodies their collective female energy, or Shakti. She is depicted riding a lion or tiger, with, in each of her eight or ten arms, a special weapon loaned to her by her male creators.

Although portrayed as beautiful, Durga also has a terrifying aspect called Kali, and, when wrathful, changes back and forth into Kali. According to the *Devi Mahatmya*, after slaying the asura Raktabija and draining him of his blood, Kali went on a rampage and by her furious dancing threatened to destroy the world. Shiva kept on calling out to her, but she could or would not hear him. At last, he threw himself under her feet, which brought her out of her trance. This arresting image of Shiva being trampled upon by a woman, the female counterpart of his own Bhairava aspect, is popular in Hindu art.

Our own Shakti is sometimes envisioned as a coiled snake [*kundalini*] lying dormant in the base of the spine, or *muladhara* [root chakra]. When gently awakened through yogic or tantric practice, the snake unfurls and rises up through the body, leading to spiritual liberation. But be warned: sudden awaking of the snake can lead to the bad kind of madness.

23

THE GUPTAS: THE GOLDEN AGE OF INDIA

The various currents so far discussed came to a head in the fifth and sixth centuries CE, leading to an 'Indian Renaissance'. Although 'Golden Age' is most often associated with the Guptas, India has, in fact, had several 'golden ages', notably under the Mauryas (Chapter 14), the Cholas (peaked ninth century CE), and the Mughals (peaked seventeenth century CE)—not to mention the IVC.

The origins of the Gupta dynasty, in the region of Magadha, are shrouded in mystery. The founder appears to have been one Sri Gupta, with 'Gupta' deriving from *gup* ['to protect'] and 'Sri' being a title of respect. At the turn of the fifth century, Sri Gupta was succeeded by his son Ghatotkacha, who was in turn succeeded by his son Chandragupta I (r. c. 319-335).

Chandragupta I—not to be confused with Chandragupta Maurya, after whom he may have been named—adopted the title of Maharajadhiraja [Great King of Kings], suggesting that he ruled over an empire. His marriage to the Licchavi princess Kumaradevi may have increased his holdings, or cemented his power—and she features alongside him on gold coins from the period. For their currency, the Guptas borrowed from the Kushans the denomination of Dinara, which derives from the Roman *Denarius aureus*.

Chandragupta was succeeded by his son Samudragupta (r. c. 335-375). Known as the 'Napoleon of India', the battle-scarred Samudragupta ['Protected by the Sea'] made many military conquests—as attested by the eulogy on the Allahabad Pillar, composed by the contemporary poet and courtier Harisena. The Allahabad Pillar also carries one of the pillar edicts of Ashoka, and an inscription by the Mughal emperor Jahangir: one pillar, two thousand years, three golden ages.

Samudragupta's empire now stretched from the Ravi to the Brahmaputra, and from the Himalayas to the Vindhyas. To mark his triumph, he performed an Ashvamedha (Chapter 2). An epitome of the ideal king, Samudragupta wrote poetry and played the *veena*, an instrument resembling the lute. Although his Nalanda and Gaya inscriptions call him *Paramabhagavata* ['Foremost among the devotees of Vishnu'], he tolerated King Sirimeghavanna of Anuradhapura [Sri Lanka] to build a Buddhist monastery and rest house at Bodhgaya.

Samudragupta was succeeded by his hapless son, Ramagupta. According to the *Devichandraguptam*, a play attributed to Vishakhadatta (fl. c. sixth century), the compromised Ramagupta surrendered his wife Dhruvadevi to the Shaka [Indo-Scythian] king. Disguised as Dhruvadevi, Ramagupta's brother Chandragupta sneaked into the enemy camp and killed the king in his sleep. In time, he deposed Ramagupta, married Dhruvadevi, and ruled as Chandragupta II (r. c. 375-415).

Chandragupta II continued to consolidate and expand the empire, notably by taking a second wife, Kuberanaga, from the Naga dynasty of Central India, and marrying his daughter Prabhavatigupta to the king of the southern Vakataka kingdom.

After the death of her husband Rudrasena II, Prabhavatigupta effectively ruled Vakataka as regent for some twenty years. Chandragupta II established a secondary capital at Ujjain, which had served as capital of the Avanti Mahajanapada, and later as capital of the Western Province of the Mauryan Empire (as a prince, Ashoka had served as Viceroy of Ujjain).

The Vaishnavite Guptas had Garuda, the vehicle of Vishnu, for their emblem: although Chandragupta II patronized Vaishnava sects, the Udayagiri inscription of his foreign minister Virasena attests to the construction of a temple dedicated to Shiva, and an inscription found at Sanchi records the donations made by his officer Amrakardava to the local Buddhist monastery. The Iron pillar of Delhi, which remains largely rust-free, attests to the technological advancement of the age.

It is in these years that Fa'hsien (d. 422), the Chinese monk in search of Buddhist manuscripts (Chapter 16), visited India, which he painted as a peaceful and prosperous land.

On reaching Mathura, Fa'hsien wrote:

> All south from this is named the Middle Kingdom. In it the cold and heat are finely tempered, and there is neither frost nor snow. The people are many and happy; they have not to register their households ... only those who cultivate the royal land have to pay [a part of] the grain from it. If they want to go, they go; if they want to stay, they stay. The king governs without decapitation or [any other] corporal punishments. Criminals are simply fined, lightly or heavily, according to the circumstances [of each case]. Even after repeated attempts at wicked rebellion, they only have their right hand cut off. The king's bodyguards and attendants all have salaries.

The legendary Vikramaditya, an ideal king who, in most accounts, ruled from Ujjain, may have been calqued, among others, on Chandragupta II—who, like many an Indian king, adopted the title of 'Vikramaditya' ['Sun of Valour', i.e. Surya]. According to lore, Vikramaditya invited nine luminaries, the *Navaratna* [Nine Gems], to reside at his court, although the scholars listed did not all live at the same time.

Still, Chandragupta may have had for court poet no less than Kalidasa, the greatest Indian writer of any age. Little is known about this 'Indian Shakespeare', and it might be that he is a composite of several court poets, or Kalidasas. His extant works include three dramas, two epic poems, and two lyric poems, inspired by the Vedas, the Itihasas, and the Puranas.

The most famous among them is the *Abhijnanashakuntala*, or *Recognition of Shakuntala*, which tells of King Dushyanta's seduction of the nymph Shakuntala, his later rejection of Shakuntala and their child, and their reunion in heaven. The child in question is none other than Bharata, ancestor of the Pandavas and Kauravas and eponym of India.

The *Prologue to the Theatre* at the beginning of *Faust* likely owes to Goethe's reading of Kalidasa's *Shakuntala*, which he lauded in a pair of couplets:

> Wouldst thou the young year's blossoms and the fruits
> of its decline
> And all by which the soul may be charmed, enraptured,
> feasted, fed,
> Wouldst thou the earth and heaven itself in one sole
> name combine?
> I name thee, O Sakuntala! and all at once is said.
>
> — JW VON GOETHE

Chandragupta II was succeeded by his son Kumaragupta (r. 415-455). Like his grandfather Samudragupta, Kumaragupta is known to have performed an Ashvamedha—suggesting that he made further conquests. He named his son Skandagupta in honour of the god of war, Kartikeya [Skanda]. He issued a large variety of coins, established diplomatic relations with the Liu Song dynasty of China, and founded the Nalanda *mahavihara* [monastic university] in Magadha.

Regarded as the world's first residential university, Nalanda attracted students from as far afield as Anatolia, Japan, and Indonesia, and played an important role in the development of Mahayana and Vajrayana Buddhism. Though Buddhistic, it offered every subject, including the Vedas. It had ten temples, eight compounds, and a great library spread across three large buildings including the nine-storey Ratnodadhi [Sea of Jewels].

In around 640, the Chinese Buddhist monk Xuanzang spent nearly two years at Nalanda, and described it thus:

> The entire establishment is surrounded by a brick wall... One gate opens into the great college, from which are separated eight other halls standing in the middle. The richly adorned towers and the fairy-like turrets, like pointed hill-tops, are grouped together. The observatories are lost in the morning vapours and the upper rooms tower above the clouds.

Some decades later, the Chinese Buddhist monk Yijing spent ten years at Nalanda, which, he claims, received the income of two hundred villages for its maintenance. The compound, he says, incorporated ten great pools, and the day began with bathing in one of the pools. Xuanzang too had described an azure pool that 'winds around the monasteries, adorned with the full-blown cups of the blue lotus...' Oxford and Harvard, eat your heart out.

Over the centuries, the Nalanda *mahavihara* followed the fortunes of Buddhism in India, before, in 1193, being raided and destroyed by Muslim invaders.

Late in his reign, Kumaragupta's empire came under threat from the Hunas. As the Hunnic hordes migrated out of the steppes, one group moved westwards towards the Volga, displacing the Goths and Alans, while another, the so-called White Huns, or Hunas, moved eastwards towards the Oxus.

In 455, Skandagupta, Kumaragupta's son by a junior wife, acceded to the throne. His Bhitari pillar inscription suggests that he restored Gupta fortunes by defeating his 'enemies', possibly the Pushyamitras, a tribe on the banks of the Narmada, or a rival claimant, or claimants, to the throne. Before or after that, he repulsed the first wave of Hunas.

The last of the great Gupta emperors, Skandagupta was succeeded, in 467, by Purugupta, his younger half-brother by Kumaragupta's chief queen. Just as the Huns played a part in the fall of the Western Roman Empire, so they contributed to the fall of the Guptas and Classical India, among others, by disrupting Indo-Roman trade. Vishnugupta, the last recognized Gupta king, reigned from 540 to 550.

At Nalanda, one of the Heads may have been the astronomer and mathematician Aryabhata (476-c. 550). In the sunset years of the Guptas, he wrote at least two works, which came to be known as the *Aryabhatiya* and the lost *Aryabhatasiddhanta* on astronomical computations. In the *Aryabhatiya*, which consists of just 108 terse verses (plus 13 introductory ones), Aryabhata treats of geometric measurements, using 3.1416 for *pi*, which he realizes is an irrational number. He defines sine, cosine, versine, and inverse sine, and, in a single sutra, supplies a table of sines. He also covers linear equations, quadratic and indeterminate equations, compound interest, and more.

Turning to astronomy, Aryabhata ascribes the luminosity of the Moon and planets to reflected sunlight, and eclipses to shadows cast by and falling upon the Earth. He calculates Earth's circumference at 24,835 miles (modern figure 24,902), and the sidereal rotation at 23 hours 56 minutes and 4.1 seconds (modern figure 23:56:4.091). In one verse, he says that the apparent westward motion of the stars owes to Earth's rotation about its axis—but in the next verse describes the motion of the stars and planets as real movements.

He gets some other things wrong. In particular, he presents a geocentric model of the solar system, with eccentric and epicyclic models of planetary motion—inspired, perhaps, by Ptolemy. His contemporary Varahamihira (c. 505-587), whose greater interest lay in astrology and divination, wrote a summary of the treatises of five schools of astronomy, the *Panchasiddhantika* [Five Doctrines], in which he discusses Greek, Egyptian, and Roman models—even supplying complete Ptolemaic charts and tables. Today, Aryabhata is commemorated in a university, a lunar crater, and India's first satellite, launched in 1975 from the USSR.

In providing algorithms for obtaining square and cubic roots, Aryabhata uses the place-value system. He also demonstrates implicit knowledge of zero. But instead of Brahmi numerals, he opts for the Vedic custom of representing numbers by letters of the alphabet. The positional base-ten 'Indo-Arabic' numeral system, and the derivative decimal numeral system, emerged in India in the sixth or seventh century. By the ninth century, it had been adopted by Arabic mathematicians. It only crossed into Europe in the twelfth century, when monks began to read Arabic. Even then, it remained largely confined to Northern Italy, until the arrival of the printing press in the fifteenth century. The ten glyphs, from zero to nine, derive from Brahmi numerals, used already in the Edicts of Ashoka.

In any positional system, it is useful, although not essential, to have a symbol for 'nothing', to represent numbers such as 100 and 1001. But the real revolution, which makes the numbers manipulable, is the realization, which occurred gradually in Gupta India, that 'nothing' is not a mere placeholder but a number in its own right. The Sanskrit *suniya* [void] became *sifr* [empty] in Arabic. Leonardo of Pisa (d. 1250), better known as Fibonacci, translated *sifr* into Latin as *zephyrum*, which became *zefiro* in Italian and *zevero* in Venetian. In around 1600, 'zero' finally entered the English language. Most of England's great cathedrals were built without it.

One of the fields of study at Nalanda was medicine, or Ayurveda ['Knowledge of life/longevity']. As in the humoralism of Hippocrates, balance is emphasized, in this case between the three *doshas* [elements], reminiscent of the three *gunas*. Suppressing natural urges is considered unhealthy, although moderation is recommended. The principal historical texts are, in order of antiquity, the *Charaka Samhita*, *Sushruta Samhita*, and *Ashtanga Hridaya*. Of the three, the most interesting is the *Sushruta Samhita*, with its impressive chapters on *shalya tantra* [surgery]. It is considered the work of the physician Sushruta ['Renowned'], who flourished in the sixth century.

Sushruta is known as the 'Father of Plastic Surgery' for his description of rhinoplasty using cheek flaps. The nose in Ancient India was seen as an organ of respect and reputation, and there was a tradition of nose amputation as a punishment for criminals and adulterous women—which is why, in the *Ramayana*, Lakshmana cuts off Shurpanakha's nose. It is even said that Ravana ordered the royal physicians to correct the defect, suggesting that rhinoplasty is older even than Sushruta. But even if he only perfected rhinoplasty, Sushruta was the first to attribute malaria to mosquitoes and link the spread of plague to rats—which, I think, are far greater achievements.

Figure 30. The temple at Bhitargaon, built in the late 5th century (and pictured in 1875), is one of the oldest surviving examples of the Nagara style of temple architecture with curved 'mountain peak', or shikhara.

The *Sushruta Samhita* details over 1,000 disease entities, 700 medicinal plants, 300 surgical procedures, and 121 surgical instruments. Other than rhinoplasty, some of the procedures described include lithotomy, cataract removal, prostate gland removal, hernia repair, and caesarean section. There is even a discussion of prosthetics limbs.

Sterility and aseptic technique are emphasized, and achieved, for example, by fumigating the operating room with certain plants extracts. For anaesthetics and sedatives, wine, cannabis, and henbane are recommended. Wounds may be stapled by the jaws of ants: once the ants have bitten at the margins, their bodies are torn off, leaving just the heads behind.

There is even considerable discussion of ethics and philosophy. Prevention is better than cure. Health is more than the mere absence of disease. Optimal health is a harmony of mind and body, achieved through rational thought, balanced nutrition, and regular exercise. A physician cannot pretend to restore others unless he is himself balanced. He should honour the patient's absolute surrender, and consider him as his own son.

I like to think that, in their spare time, Aryabhata and Sushruta played chaturanga, the ancestor of chess, which, by the sixth century, had become widespread. Played on an eight-by-eight uncheckered board, chaturanga ['four divisions': elephantry, chariotry, cavalry, and infantry] had different pieces with different powers, the objective being to capture the opponent's *raja* or reduce the opponent's pieces to just the *raja*. Over the centuries, the *mantri* [advisor] or *senapati* [general] became the queen, the *gaja* [elephant] became the bishop, and the *ratha* [chariot] became the rook. Remarkably, the *raja*, *ratha*, *ashva* [horse], and *padati* [foot soldier] moved the same as their modern equivalents, the king, rook, knight, and pawn, although the *padati* did not have a double-step option on the first move.

For the story, in around 700, the Persians introduced the notion of warning that the *raja* [*shah*] was under attack to prevent an early or accidental end to a game. Later, they added the rule that the *shah* could not be moved into check or left in check, meaning that he could no longer be captured but only made helpless [*shah mat*]. Chess, in the intermediary form of Shatranj, entered Europe in the tenth century, probably through Islamic Spain. Mediaeval players considered it nobler to win by checkmate, so that annihilation became only a half-win before altogether disappearing, in around 1600.

24

THE SIX DARSHANAS: SAMKHYA-YOGA

A *darshana* [from *drish*, 'to see, to experience'] is an outlook, a philosophy, literally, a 'vision'. One of India's largest broadcasters is called Doordarshan, or 'Distant Vision'—reminiscent of the gift of divine vision [*divya drishti*] which enabled Sanjaya to witness the Mahabharata War from afar and relate it to the blind Dhritarashtra.

The term *darshana* is especially associated with the six orthodox [*astika*] schools of Indian philosophy, the so-called *shaddarshana*, or 'six visions'. What makes them orthodox, and therefore Hindu, is that they accept the authority of the Vedas (or, at least, do not explicitly reject it), as well as the existence of Atman. With good reason, the *shaddarshana* are often presented in pairs: Samkhya-Yoga, Nyaya-Vaisheshika (Chapter 25), and Mimamsa-Vedanta (Chapter 26).

In contrast, systems that reject the authority of the Vedas are called *nastika*, or heterodox. They include Buddhism, Jainism, Charvaka, Ajivika, Ajnana, and others. I have already covered the *nastika* schools, especially in Chapters 9, 10, 11, and 13—leaving us only to treat of the *astika*.

The *astika* schools developed in large part in reaction to the threat and challenge of the *nastika* schools, especially Buddhism—making this, I think, the right order in which to cover them. Moreover, keeping the technical *astika* schools for last, on the background of the history of Indian thought, means that they are now more likely to make sense.

The founder of the Samkhya school is held to be Kapila ['the Red One'], who lived, perhaps, in the sixth century BCE. Very little is known about him. He is sometimes described as an avatar of Vishnu or grandson of Brahma. He is mentioned by Krishna in the *Bhagavad Gita* [10.26] as the greatest of sages: 'Amongst the *gandharvas* I am Chitrath, and among the *siddhas* I am sage Kapil.' According to Puranic lore, his meditation produced such intense inner heat [*tapas*] that, when they disturbed him, he incinerated the Sagarputras, the 60,001 sons of King Sagara, simply by opening his eyes.

Some of Kapila's teachings are quoted in the *Bhagavata Purana*, for example:

> 'When one is completely cleansed of the impurities of lust and greed produced from the false identification of the body as 'I' and bodily possessions as 'mine', one's mind becomes purified. In that pure state he transcends the stage of so-called material happiness and distress' [3.25.16].

In the Buddhist tradition, it was the students of Kapila who built the Shakya capital of Kapilavastu. Siddhartha Gautama, who was raised in the city (Chapter 9), was therefore steeped in Samkhya philosophy—explaining the affinities or similarities between Samkhya and Buddhism.

Kapila is held to have authored the *Samkhya* (or *Kapila*) *Sutra*, although the extant text appears to be mediaeval in origin. Instead, the school's primary text is the *Samkhyakarika* by Ishvarakrishna, who lived in the third or fourth century CE.

The *Samkhyakarika* consists of 72 shlokas written in the *arya* metre, which consists of four *padas* [lines]. Unusually, the arya metre is based on the number of *matras* [morae] per pada, with a structure of 12, 18, 12, and 15—making it sound very musical. In the *Samkhyakarika*, Ishvarakrishna describes himself as the successor of the disciples of Kapila, and claims also to be outlining the lost *Sashtitantra* [Science of Sixty Topics]. In the first verse, he states the aim of Samkhya: to eliminate the three forms of *dukkha*, or suffering: internal, from physical and mental disease; external, from outside threats, especially other people; and divine, that is, from natural disasters.

Samkhya is a radical dualism, in holding that the universe is made up of two independent, infinite, and eternal realities: *Purusha* (souls) and *Prakriti* (matter or nature). The Purushas, or Atmas, must be many for the law of karma to operate. The Purushas are conscious, but have no attributes; they are pure 'witness consciousness'. Prakriti is composed of the three *gunas*, *sattva*, *rajas*, and *tamas*. Initially, the gunas are in equilibrium. But at its approach, Purusha disturbs this equilibrium in favour of rajas, and this imbalance sets off material creation.

Unlike Western dualism, which is between mind and matter, Samkhyan dualism is between self and matter—with 'matter' encompassing most of what Westerners would consider 'mind' (intellect, ego, emotions...), everything, in fact, but witness consciousness, of which mind is the instrument. Also unlike Western dualism, Samkhyan dualism is atheistic or agnostic. Although an orthodox school, Samkhya is remarkably silent about God, the Vedas, and the Brahmanas.

At the approach of Purusha, undifferentiated [*Mula*] Prakriti evolves 23 *tattvas* [elements, aspects], first *buddhi* [intelligence], and from buddhi *ahamkara* [ego or self-consciousness]. Under the influence of sattva guna, ahamkara yields the five organs of sense (eyes, ears, nose, skin, tongue), the five organs of action (arms, legs, speech, organs of elimination, organs of creation), and *manas* [mind]. Then, under the influence of tamas guna, ahamkara yields the five subtle elements (sight, hearing, smell, touch, taste), from which the five material elements (earth, air, water, fire, ether) emerge.

Notice that the material world is last in the order of creation. That it is evolved from the five senses suggests that the world is an illusion, although this is never explicitly stated. Manas has a special role, which is to mediate between the ten organs, the five senses, and the world without. Being of Prakriti, buddhi, ahamkara, and manas are not conscious. However, they appear to be conscious, and are set into motion, by proximity with Purusha—functioning, as it were, by reflected consciousness.

Adding Purusha and Prakriti to the 23 tattvas makes a total of 25 tattvas—of which 24 are of Prakriti. Nonetheless, it is for the sake of Purusha that the differentiation occurs, to provide it with experience and, in time, with liberation. By reflecting the consciousness of Purusha, Prakriti is showing Purusha to itself.

Here, the *Samkhyakarika* provides a couple of analogies. As milk flows, naturally, for the growth of the calf, so Prakriti flows for the growth of Purusha.

Purusha and Prakriti are like a lame man and a blind man, lost in the wilderness. The blind man carries the lame man, who guides his steps. Both are looking for their way home, to *moksha*, when they will part ways. But having never travelled, the lame man is avid of experience, and is so enthralled by his adventure that he forgets about his destination.

Implicit in this model of evolution, in which everything comes out of something else, is the Samkhya theory of causation. Like Parmenides, Kapila and Ishvarakrishna held that, because something cannot come out of nothing, the effect must already be present in the cause. There is, strictly speaking, no creation or destruction in the Samkhyan model of the universe—and, therefore, no need for a Creator.

In terms of epistemology, Samkhya admits of three *pramanas* (reliable means of knowledge): direct sense perception, logical inference, and reliable testimony, in that order. Because direct sense perception is unphilosophical, liberation depends on the other two pramanas, especially inference—which is the work of buddhi, or intelligence.

To be compatible with the law of karma, Samkhya assumes that a Purusha that is bonded to Prakriti (that is, a *jiva*) has two bodies: a gross, mortal body, and a subtle body made up of the higher functions which transmigrates according to past merit. The continuity of the subtle body enables the Purusha to keep on learning through numerous incarnations.

Final liberation consists in the realization of the separateness of Purusha and Prakriti. The jiva then passes from ignorance [*avidya*] to knowledge [*viveka*], and from bondage [*bandhana*] to isolation [*kaivalya*] and freedom [*moksha*].

This involves a process of involution, or 'going back to the womb' [*prati-prasava*]—that is, reversing, through intellect and understanding, the process of evolution, from the material elements back to Mula Prakriti and beyond.

In short, as every child has intuited, final liberation consists in counting backwards.

Samkhya exercised such a profound influence on Yoga that the two schools are often referred to collectively as Samkhya-Yoga. But whereas Samkhya emphasizes knowledge as the path to liberation, Yoga rather emphasizes discipline.

Although Yoga essentially borrows the metaphysics of Samkhya, it introduces a twenty-sixth tattva, namely, Ishvara, or 'the Lord'—for which reason it has been called Seshvara-Samkhya, or 'theistic Samkhya'. The meaning of 'Ishvara' is open to interpretation, but it may be regarded as a special Purusha which is unentangled and therefore inactive.

Although the Rig Veda already suggests the presence of yogi-like ascetics, the earliest discussions of yoga [from *yuj*, 'to join', 'to yoke', 'to unite'] are to be found in the Upanishads (Chapter 7). In the Kathopanishad [2.3], Yama defines yoga for Nachiketa as the holding back of the senses and stilling of the intellect. In the *Bhagavad Gita* [4.3], Krishna calls the knowledge of yoga 'ancient'. He outlines three yogas, or paths to moksha: Jnana Yoga, the Path of Knowledge; Karma Yoga, the Path of (selfless) Action; and Bhakti Yoga, the Path of Devotion. Yoga is also a central concept in Buddhism and Jainism.

In the second century BCE, or perhaps the fifth century CE, Patanjali collected the ideas around yoga in the *Yoga Sutra*. These 196 verses became the foundational text of Yoga, which, towards the end of the first millennium, began to be mentioned as a separate school. Patanjali's synthesis influenced all other schools of Hindu philosophy, which regard it as authoritative. It is sometimes referred to as Raja Yoga [Royal Yoga] or Ashtanga Yoga [Eight-Limbed Yoga] to distinguish it from the many other forms of yoga, such as Jnana, Karma, Bhakti, Mantra, and Tantra—which are, it should be stressed, more complementary than mutually exclusive.

Patanjali, who is sometimes regarded as an avatar of the serpent Shesha, is also held to have written the *Mahabhashya*, or Great Commentary on Panini's Grammar (Chapter 4), as well as a treatise on medicine, the *Patanjalatantra*. However, the *Yoga Sutra* and *Mahabhashya* are very different in content, language, and style, with no cross-references from the one to the other. Even the contents of the *Yoga Sutra* appear to span several centuries, suggesting that the original work may have been supplemented. As often with Ancient Indian authors, 'Patanjali' may be more than one person.

The *Yoga Sutra* has four sections: *Samadhi* [Concentration], *Sadhana* [Practice], *Vibhuti* [Yogic or Magical Powers], and *Kaivalya* [Isolation or Liberation]. In the first section, Patanjali defines yoga as 'the cessation of mental fluctuations' [*chitta vritti nirodha*]—with *chitta* [mind] assimilated, in the Samkhyan system, to buddhi, ahamkara, and manas. In the third section, he warns against practicing yoga for the perverted purpose of acquiring yogic powers—suggesting that this sort of thing may have been common. The first extant commentary on the *Yoga Sutra* is by no less of an authority than the legendary Vyasa (Chapter 20), so that 'the *Yoga Sutra* of Patanjali' ought really to be understood as 'the *Yoga Sutra* of Patanjali, as expanded and interpreted by Vyasa'.

The eight limbs or stages of Patanjali's Yoga are:

1. *Yama* [abstinence or restraint]
2. *Niyama* [discipline or observances]
3. *Asana* ['seat', posture]
4. *Pranayama* [breath control]
5. *Pratyahara* [withdrawal of the senses]
6. *Dharana* [concentration of the mind on some object]
7. *Dhyana* [steady meditation on that object]
8. *Samadhi* [absorption, ecstatic union with the ultimate]

The first two stages are ethical preparations. Yama involves: non-injury or non-violence [*ahimsa*], truthfulness [*satya*], non-stealing [*asteya*], chastity [*brahmacharya*], and non-possession [*aparigraha*]. Niyama involves: purity or cleanliness [*shaucha*], contentment [*santosa*], austerity [*tapas*], study [*svadhyaya*], and devotion to God [*Ishvara-pranidhana*].

The next two stages are physical preparations, in each case, involving a series of exercises aimed at removing physical or bodily distractions. The fifth stage involves taking control of the mind by emptying it of impressions. The remaining three stages, which may take several lifetimes to perfect, aim at increasingly heightened states of awareness and return.

According to Patanjali, the five *kleshas* [poisons, obstacles to Yoga] are: ignorance [*avidya*], ego [*asmita*], attachment or desire [*raga*], aversion to unpleasant things or truths [*dvesha*], and fear of death and desire to live [*abhinivesha*].

The aim of yoga, and ascetic practice in general, is essentially to react against ordinary human habits, which entangle us, or our Purusha, with Prakriti, to the extent that Purusha identifies with Prakriti and more particularly with the restless chitta and its manifold modifications.

This is a far cry from the yoga practised in the West as a form of physical culture, with postures borrowed from Hatha Yoga and optional spiritual sprinkling for stress relief. Even Hatha Yoga is about a lot more than that.

25

THE SIX DARSHANAS: NYAYA-VAISHESHIKA

The Nyaya school developed out of the Ancient Indian tradition of debate [*vada*], including the dialectic tournaments held in kingly courts and Vedic colleges.

An original concern with argumentation, or *nyaya* ['method', 'rules', 'logic'], led, over the centuries, to the development of a broader philosophy and soteriology [doctrine of salvation], completing the transformation from body of knowledge into philosophical school. Just as Yoga adopts the metaphysics of Samkhya, so Nyaya adopts the metaphysics of Vaisheshika. From the tenth century, Nyaya and Vaisheshika began to be spoken of as a single school.

Nyaya-Vaisheshika shares many of the aims of Samkhya-Yoga. If right knowledge leads to successful action, it also leads to virtuous action, since (echoing Socrates) vice is always the outcome of some confusion. Thus, bondage and suffering result from ignorance and misapprehension, while liberation is brought about by right knowledge.

Logic, my friends, can save your soul.

To an extent, Nyaya evolved in reaction to Buddhist skepticism. Having developed a sophisticated system of reasoning, Nyaya scholars (or Naiyanikas) used it to prove the existence of the things denied and undermined by Buddhism, first among them, God and the soul.

For example:

> Things like desires and feelings are qualities.
> All qualities inhere in substances.
> Therefore, things like desires and feelings must inhere in a substance.

Renowned for the rigour of its argumentation, and especially for its treatment of inference, Nyaya influenced all other schools of Hindu philosophy, as well as Buddhism. I see many similarities with Aristotle's logic and rhetoric, such as finding analogies, using examples, and considering counterarguments.

Some time between the sixth century BCE and the second century CE, Aksapada Gautama distilled and systematized the knowledge of argumentation in the *Nyaya Sutra*, which became the foundational text of Nyaya. Nothing is known about Aksapada Gautama. The *Nyaya Sutra* may have been added to over the centuries, with Aksapada Gautama being the first and main author. The earliest extant commentary, by Paksilasvamin Vatsyayana (fifth century CE or second century BCE), itself attracted many secondary and tertiary commentaries.

The *Nyaya Sutra*, which consists of 528 verses, is divided into five books, each with two chapters. Much of the work is devoted to the sixteen categories [*padarthas*] listed in the first verse of the first chapter of the first book:

> Perfection is attained by the correct knowledge of the true nature of sixteen categories: means of right knowledge [*pramana*]; objects of right knowledge [*prameya*]; doubt [*samsaya*]; purpose [*prayojana*]; familiar instance [or example, *drishtanta*]; established tenet [or conclusion, *siddhanta*]; members of an inference [*avayava*]; [hypothetical] reasoning [*tarka*]; ascertainment of results [or settlement, *nirnaya*]; discussion [or debate, *vada*]; sophistic disputations [*jalpa*]; cavil [or destructive debate, *vitanda*]; fallacies [*hetvabhasa*]; quibbles [or equivocation, *chala*]; futile rejoinders [or misleading objections, *jati*]; and ways of losing an argument [or clinchers, *nigrahasthana*].
>
> — NYAYA SUTRA 1.1.1

Knowledge of these sixteen categories, acquired by debate, contemplation, and yoga, leads to liberation and salvation. The first two categories, *pramana* and *prameya*, are so central as to fill Books 2 and 3. Interestingly, a section of Book 4 [4.1.19-21] appears to reject the hypothesis of God or Ishvara, although later Naiyanikas offered nine proofs for God's existence—and argued, predominantly by the principle of parsimony, that God could only be one. Book 5, which may be a later addition, presents 24 futile rejoinders and 22 ways of losing an argument.

The four *pramanas*, or accurate means of knowledge, are: perception [*pratyaksha*], inference [*anumana*], comparison or analogy [*upamana*], and reliable testimony [*sabda*]. The twelve *prameyas*, or valid objects of knowledge, are: soul, body, sense organs, sense objects, intellect, mind [*manas*], activity, fault, transmigration, fruit, suffering, and liberation. Of the four pramanas, anumana, upamana, and sabda all ultimately rely on pratyaksha, which is the primary means of knowledge.

But even knowledge obtained through pratyaksha can be invalid, and there is much discussion of the criteria of validity. According to Gautama, a perceptual cognition 'arises from the connection between sense faculty and object, is not dependent on words, is non-deviating, and is determinate' [1.1.4].

Manas—which, remember, is not the soul—is also a sense faculty, albeit an internal one. Naiyanikas came to recognize three means or modes of 'extraordinary perception', essentially, memory, induction, and intuition or yogic perception.

Inference, says Gautama, is of three kinds: 'a priori [from cause to effect], a posteriori [from effect to cause], and commonly seen' [1.1.5]. In debate, inference requires a formal five-step procedure, for example:

1. There is fire on the hill.
2. Because there is smoke on the hill.
3. Wherever there is smoke, there is fire—like a kitchen hearth and unlike a lake.
4. There is smoke on the hill.
5. Therefore, there is fire on the hill.

In this example, fire is the *sadhya* [major term], the hill is the *paksha* [minor term], and smoke is the *hetu* [middle term]. In the statement of the rule (step 3, the *udaharana*), it is expected to provide an example, and sometimes also a negative example, or *vipaksha*. In practice, the fourth and fifth steps, the *upanaya* [application] and *nigamana* [conclusion], are often left out.

Being a method of scientific inquiry, Indian logic cannot be divorced from content. Compared to Western formal or symbolic logic, there is less of a distinction between deduction and induction, and validity and soundness. Because premises must be true, the method of indirect proof is not recognized.

Nyaya is a robust realism. Reality, including universals, the soul, and God, is out there to be discovered and known. Knowledge is always possible: if there is a difficulty, it is not with reality, or with the means of knowledge, but with us as enquirers. Although radically anti-skeptical, Nyaya does recognize that doubt can be an instigator of knowledge. Radical doubt, however, would undermine our ability to achieve our secular and spiritual aims—which was the whole point of the exercise.

Vaisheshika [from *vishesha*, 'distinction', 'particularity'] is concerned with categories of being, that is, with the kinds of things that are. It sets out to identify, classify, and analyse the various components of reality and their relations.

Unusually, and unexpectedly, for an Indian system, Vaisheshika is an atomism, which holds that reality is made up of indivisible and imperceptible atoms. But unlike Buddhist atomism, it is also a realism, which holds that the objects of perception, although made up of atoms, add up to something more than the sum of their parts. And unlike Greek atomism, that is, the atomism of Democritus and Leucippus, it admits of such things as souls, karma, and God.

Vaisheshika complements the Nyaya account of knowledge with an account of the objects of knowledge. In fact, it is thought to be more ancient than Nyaya, and more ancient, perhaps, than Buddhism—since the *Vaisheshika Sutra* makes no mention of Buddhism or Buddhist doctrines. It may have been influenced by those other atomists, the Ajivikas and Charvakas, or influenced them. Although Vaisheshika later admitted of God, there is no mention of God in the *Vaisheshika Sutra*.

By the eleventh century, Nyaya and Vaisheshika had so much in common as to merge into Nyaya-Vaisheshika. For example, both assimilated knowledge with the knowledge of causes, while denying the Samkhya and Vedanta doctrine that an effect pre-exists in its cause. Still, there remained some points of difference. Vaisheshika, like Buddhism, only admitted of perception and inference as valid means of knowledge, whereas Nyaya also admitted of comparison and reliable testimony.

The founder or synthesizer of Vaisheshika is Kanada [from *kana*, grain or particle], so called because he survived on a diet of gleaned grain. Fittingly, 'Kanada' can also mean 'atom eater'. Little is known about the man, not even when he lived, with estimates ranging from the sixth century BCE to the fourth century CE. The *Vaisheshika Sutra*, also known as the *Kanada Sutra*, consists of around four hundred verses, divided into ten books, each with two chapters. Since many of the verses are ambiguous, students rely instead on the 'commentary' (in fact a derivative work) by Prashastapada, who lived maybe in the sixth century.

Vaisheshika begins by classifying the objects of experience into six categories: substance [*dravya*], quality [*guna*], action or activity [*karma*], generality [*samanya*], particularity [*vishesha*, the etymological root of Vaisheshika], and inherence [*samavaya*]. Later, a seventh category, absence [*abhava*, or non-existence], came to be included. Although non-being is discussed in the *Vaisheshika Sutra*, Kanada did not grant it the status of a category, or *padartha* ['word meaning'].

The first three padarthas, substance, quality, and action, are perceivable, whereas the remainder are products of intellectual discrimination. Notice that *dravya*, *guna*, and *karma* correspond, respectively, to noun, adjective, and verb—pointing to the continued influence of grammar over Indian philosophy.

Discussion of categories such as substance, quality, action or causation, generality, and particularity is reminiscent of Greek philosophy, especially Aristotle's *Physics* and *Metaphysics* and Plato's Theory of the Forms.

Substance, as the substratum in which quality and activity inhere, is the primary category. According to Vaisheshika, there are nine eternal substances: earth, water, fire, air (or wind), ether [akasha], time, space, spirit, and mind. The first five substances are *bhutas*, or elements, and may initially have corresponded to the five senses. Whereas atomic substances (earth, water, fire, and air) are eternal and indestructible, compound substances, that is, objects, are transient. Mind too is considered atomic, although non-combinatorial. Mind, the internal sense, is therefore imperceptible—and cannot give rise, at any one time, to more than one experience. Whereas souls are innumerable, ether, time, and space are only one in number, and all-pervasive. It is through mind, and therefore through the body, that the soul comes to know itself and the world. Because the self is not possessed of consciousness during deep sleep, consciousness is not an essential attribute of the soul. Which begs the question, what is the soul without mind and the body that comes with it?

Quality, as has been said, inheres in substance. But although 'red' cannot exist outside of substance, it can be conceived and named independently—which is why quality qualifies as a category. Kanada identified seventeen qualities, including a few psychological ones: colour, taste, smell, touch, number, size, individuality, conjunction, disjunction, priority, posteriority, knowledge, pleasure, pain, desire, aversion, and effort. To these, Prashastapada added seven more: heaviness, fluidity, viscosity, merit, demerit, sound, and faculty.

Activity is the cause of conjunction and disjunction. There are five kinds of activity: upward movement, downward movement, contraction, expansion, and locomotion. Both quality and activity inhere in substance, quality permanently, activity only transiently. Although they are substances, ether, time, space, and spirit do not admit of activity.

Generality is akin to the Greek concept of the universal. For instance, 'Cowness' is what makes all cows a cow. It is an eternal essence, and not dependent on the existence of any cow. The highest universal is that of existence. Particularity is what distinguishes one eternal substance from another. It does not operate at the level of objects, which can be distinguished by their parts, but at the level of their atoms. Every atom, though part-less, has its own particularity. Inherence is the relation or connection between things that are inseparably connected, such as the cow and its horns, the cow and its colour, the cow and the form of 'cowness'. Inherence is what enables a cow to be something more than the sum of its parts.

Although absence or non-existence is relative and negative, yet it can be cognized, and grant knowledge. Four types of absence are recognized: antecedent absence, as when a pot has been made; subsequent absence, as when the pot has been destroyed; absolute absence, as when a thing cannot possibly be in that location, for example, fire in the sea; and mutual absence, as when one thing is not another.

All physical objects consist of combinations of spherical atoms of earth, water, fire, and air. Atoms first combine to form dyads, which then combine into visible triads (three pairs). But atoms, though the material cause, are inherently motionless. They are put into motion by the will of God, the efficient cause, to form a world that accords with the moral deserts of individual souls.

Thus it is that we get the world we deserve.

26

THE SIX DARSHANAS: MIMAMSA-VEDANTA

Mimamsa ['investigation', 'analysis'], the school of Vedic exegesis, grew out of the Vedic tradition of elucidation and interpretation. It is perhaps the oldest of the *darshanas*, or, at least, the one with the earliest antecedents. As Vedic ritualism came under increasing threat from asceticism and theism or devotionalism, it became increasingly turned to defending the Vedic worldview and way of life.

Mimamsa is concerned with the older ritual layers of the Vedas, known as the *Karma Kanda*—as opposed to the *Jnana Kanda*, or Upanishads. For this reason, it is also known as Purva-Mimamsa [Prior Study] or Karma-Mimamsa [Study of Actions].

The school that is concerned with the Jnana Kanda is, of course, Vedanta, also known as Uttara-Mimamsa [Posterior Study] or Jnana-Mimamsa [Study of Knowledge]. Whereas Purva-Mimamsa focuses on dharma, Uttara-Mimamsa focuses on Brahman. Thus Purva-Mimamsa is also known as Dharma-Mimamsa, and Uttara-Mimasa as Brahma-Mimamsa.

Although eclipsed by Vedanta, Mimamsa is the only other darshana to have survived into contemporary Hinduism. Its methods of textual analysis and interpretation have influenced every other field of study in India, not least the law.

The foundational text of Mimamsa is the *Mimamsa Sutra* of Jaimini, who lived in around the second century BCE. Jaimini may have been the student of Badarayana, author of the *Brahma Sutra*, also known as the *Vedanta Sutra*. Certainly, both philosophers quote and respond to each other, sometimes in agreement and sometimes not. According to the *Brahmanda Purana* [1.4.21], Jaimini was a student of Vyasa, to whom the *Brahma Sutra* is also attributed—although in this case 'Vyasa' ['Compiler'] may refer to Badarayana.

The *Mimamsa Sutra* consists of twelve chapters, further divided into sixty sections. It contains a total of 2745 sutras, compared to the 555 of the *Brahma Sutra* and the 72 of the *Samkhya Sutra*. The oldest extant commentary is by Shabarasvamin or Shabara, dated to around the sixth century CE. In around the seventh century, the *Shabarabhashya* was in turn commented upon by Kumarila Bhatta and Prabhakara Misra, who are considered the founders of the two most important sub-schools, the Bhatta (or Kumarila) and the Prabhakara. Among their differences is their view of language and semantics: for the Bhatta, the meaning of a sentence can only be grasped after having understood the meaning of its component words, whereas for the Prabhakara, words only acquire their meaning from their context, or syntactic relation within the sentence.

The *Mimamsa Sutra* begins, 'Now the investigation of dharma.' Beyond ritual, dharma extends to things like duties, customs, and social relations. Because dharma cannot be known by human means such as perception and inference, one must turn instead to the Vedas.

Although apprehended by sages and seers, the Vedas are eternal and authorless. Since they are part of the fabric of the universe, higher, even, than any god, they are utterly infallible. Although they contain many contradictions, imprecisions, and repetitions, these can all be accounted for, for example, by imputing them to the human, and therefore fallible, seers and sages. Sanskrit is no ordinary language. It is the emanation of Being in sound. And like the Vedas, it is eternal—its words, not mere conventions, but universals. If the remembered texts have any authority, it is because they derive it from the revealed texts, that is, from the Vedas. The other Hindu schools are misguided, but most misguided of all are the Buddhists and Jains who put their faith in supposedly omniscient beings such as the Buddha and Mahavira. To find happiness and salvation, all one need do is follow the Vedas, to the letter, to follow the dharma.

Astonishingly for this most orthodox of schools, Mimamsa denies the existence of God. The Vedas had no author, the universe no creator. The universe is eternal, and not subject to creation or dissolution. According to some Mimamsakas, Vedic gods are no more than figurative vehicles of praise and sacrifice. This atheism served Mimamsa in opposing asceticism and, especially, devotionalism, although one mediaeval sub-school, Seshvara Mimamsa [Theistic Mimamsa], did admit of God.

Instead of mysticism and skepticism, their reliance on the Vedas led the Mimamsakas to a radical realism and empiricism. All cognitions are *prima facie* valid, until and unless they can be demonstrated to be defective. As the Vedas have no author, they cannot be defective, and are therefore valid. For Prabhakara, all cognitions are unconditionally valid: it is only in judgements about them that error can occur. As well as the four of Nyaya, Mimamsa admitted of two more *pramanas*, pre-conception or postulation [*arthapatti*, derivation from circumstances] and absence or non-existence [*anupalabdhi*].

If the Vedas imply the reality of the world, they also imply the Law of Karma and immortality of the soul, or souls. The soul is the substratum of consciousness. However, consciousness is not an essential property of the soul. Instead, it only arises from association with the body, and only when the external or internal organs of knowledge are engaged. At other times, the soul only has potentiality for consciousness and knowledge. Any action produces an unseen potency [*apurva*] in the soul of the agent. By carrying out the actions prescribed in the Vedas, and refraining from those proscribed, the soul finds happiness in heaven [*svarga*]. In keeping with the times, or capitulating to them, some later Mimamsakas replaced the notion of svarga with that of moksha.

Vedanta [*Veda* + *anta*, 'End of the Vedas', or 'Essence of the Vedas'], also known as Uttara-Mimamsa ['Posterior Study'], both complements and supersedes Purva-Mimamsa. Originally, 'Vedanta' referred simply to the Upanishads, before being extended, in the mediaeval period, to the school or schools of Upanishadic exegesis.

Because its subject is Brahman, Vedanta is also called Brahma-Mimamsa. Although associated with the Upanishads, the notion of Brahman is rooted in the Rig Veda, according to which the universe was created by sacrificing a single cosmic man, Purusha.

As well as the *mukhya* Upanishads, that is, the oldest and most authoritative Upanishads, Vedanta also embraces the *Brahma Sutra* and *Bhagavad Gita* (Chapter 21), which may be looked upon as Upanishadic materials. Vedantins collectively refer to the *mukhya* Upanishads, *Brahma Sutra*, and *Bhagavad Gita* as the *Prasthanatraya*, or 'Three Sources'.

The *Brahma Sutra*, also known as the *Vedanta Sutra*, seeks to harmonize the diverse and often contradictory Upanishadic teachings on Brahman. Its 555 verses are attributed to Badarayana, the presumed teacher of Jaimini, who, we have said, lived in around the second century BCE. In the *Brahma Sutra*, Jaimini's position is—appropriately enough—presented as the original view, or *purva paksha* [former opinion], to be improved upon by Badarayana's more considered view, or *siddhanta* [settled opinion]. Badarayana quotes several Vedantic teachers, suggesting that he is, at least in part, synthesizing an already existing body of knowledge.

Vedanta's sub-schools align according to the relation that they see between Brahman and everything else, especially Atman and Ishvara. The three major sub-schools are Advaita (monism: Brahman and Atman are identical), Vishishtadvaita (qualified non-dualism), and Dvaita (dualism). Their founding gurus, respectively, Adi Shankara, Ramanuja, and Madhva, each wrote commentaries on the *Prasthanatraya*.

Whereas Advaita advocates meditation and self-knowledge as the path to salvation, Vishishtadvaita and Dvaita are related to Vaishnavism and emphasize devotion to Ishvara in the form of Vishnu and his avatars. Western notions of Hinduism are much more aligned with Advaita than with Vishishtadvaita or Dvaita.

For all their differences, the Vedantic schools all share a belief in Brahman, Atman, karma, samsara, and moksha. They all de-emphasize ritual, while upholding the Vedas, and especially the Upanishads and Aranyakas, as the only reliable means of knowledge [*pramana*] for spiritual matters. For mundane matters, Advaita admits of the same six pramanas as Mimamsa, whereas Vishishtadvaita and Dvaita accept only perception, inference, and reliable testimony.

Shankara, who flourished in the eighth century CE, wrote the earliest surviving commentary on the *Brahma Sutra*. In his commentaries, he mentions many precursors, including Gaudapada, author or compiler of the earliest extant treatise on Advaita, known as the *Mandukyakarika* (a *karika*, as opposed to a *bhashya*, is a commentary in verse, in this case on the short Mandukya Upanishad). Shankara calls Gaudapada *paramaguru* ['highest teacher'], suggesting that Gaudapada may have been the teacher of his teacher, Govinda. The fourth and last book of the *Mandukyakarika*, which may have been a later addition, is heavily influenced by Mahayana Buddhism, to the extent that it employs Buddhist terminology. Although he attacked Buddhist doctrines, Shankara is often accused of being a 'Buddhist in disguise', notably for his rejection of reality and emphasis on independent self-knowledge. He is said, in Buddhist fashion, to have founded four monasteries in the four corners of India—which may have helped to spread his teachings.

The oldest Vedantic school, Advaita ['Not two'], represents an extreme and purist position in arguing that Brahman alone is real. The self and the world are within Brahman, with any apparent difference arising from illusion [*maya*] and ignorance [*avidya*]. It is as with a rope, which seems to be a snake, or a seashell, which seems to be of silver. This world is like the foam on the sea, or a peacock's egg, created simply for play [*lila*]. Since Brahman is all, Brahman is without attributes. When the mind, which is given to maya, tries to conceive of Brahman, it sees Ishvara in one of his many forms. If certain Upanishadic statements appear to be theistic, it is because their author (nominally, Brahman) is catering to his audience. Only in deep sleep, when we are no longer dreaming, might we experience something of the formlessness of Brahman. We are then pure, disengaged consciousness, like the sun after it has set. This is the experience of disembodied Atma, of death, of home.

While grinding lenses to make ends meet, Baruch Spinoza (d. 1677) independently and rationally developed a pantheism similar to Advaita, in which the distinction between God and creation is denied, to the extent that Spinoza can speak of them interchangeably: *Deus sive Natura*, 'God or Nature.'

Ramanuja, the chief proponent of Vishishtadvaita [Qualified non-dualism], flourished in the eleventh century. Being of a dualistic disposition, he disagreed with his teacher Yamuna, who belonged to a more monistic Vedantic tradition (possibly Advaita or Bhedabheda). His commentary on the *Brahma Sutra* is known as the *Shribhashya*, or *Beautiful Commentary*.

Like man, God has both soul and body, and the world is his body. Thus, the soul and the world are modes, or attributes, of Brahman. The liberated soul becomes similar to, although not identical with, Brahman. Just as the goal of the body is to serve the soul, so the goal of individual souls is to serve God, in his personified form of Vishnu. Moksha is to be found not only in liberation from samsara, but also in the contemplation of God. By integrating devotion into his soteriology, Ramanuja gave *bhakti* a philosophical basis in Vedanta and the Vedas.

In later generations, a schism developed over the importance of God's grace in the quest for salvation. For the northern Vadakalai, also known as the Monkey school, God's grace is essential, but we must still make every effort, like a baby monkey, who must hold fast onto its mother. For the southern Tenkalai, also known as the Cat school, God's grace alone suffices, so long as we submit to it, like a kitten, who goes limp when picked up by its mother.

Madhva, the founder of Dvaita [Dualism], flourished some hundred years after Ramanuja. In some of his works, he proclaims himself to be an avatar of the wind god Vayu, whom he looked upon as a son of Vishnu.

Madhva's standout work is the *Anuvyakhyana*, a secondary commentary or metacommentary on his own commentary of the *Brahma Sutra*, in which he criticizes other sub-schools of Vedanta, especially Advaita and Vishishtadvaita.

Brahman, individual souls, and matter are separate entities. God is perfect and unalterable: while he is the efficient cause of the universe, he cannot be the material cause. Salvation comes from devotion to God, which Madhva, like Ramanuja before him, envisioned as Vishnu. However, not all souls are salvable: some are forever bound in samsara; some, even, are eternally damned in Naraka—which, according to some later Dvaitins, might suit them just fine.

Mediaeval *bhakti* movements seeking for philosophical grounding in Vedic orthodoxy found a ready partner in Dvaita, or dualistic Vedanta—which, though a sub-school of Vedanta, is much further from Advaita than, say, Samkhya.

FINAL WORDS

What came, relatively late, to be called Hinduism is a synthesis of various cultures and traditions that evolved over thousands of years.

Having no founding prophet, single book, or central authority, Hinduism is more like the Greek and Roman religions than Christianity and Islam. But unlike these ancient religions, it is still very much alive, for having adapted to the times.

Hinduism has succeeded like no other in marrying high and low, to encompass not two but several degrees of divinity: the Absolute Brahman, personal gods such as Vishnu and Shiva, their incarnations such as Krishna and Rama, other deities and sages, and natural forces and spirits.

It achieved this by maintaining an unusual degree of openness. Historically, the highly confident Hindus did not have a problem with other creeds, or even with atheism, but only with *adharma*, or lawlessness. Thus, Hindus have never been bent on proselytising and converting others to their faith, or faiths.

Their long tradition of kindness and tolerance, shared with the Buddhists and Jains and reflected in the pan-Indian doctrines of non-violence and vegetarianism, is rooted in the core concept of Atman-Brahman. There is nothing more Hindu, or more profoundly religious, than to see your neighbour, or even your neighbour's cow, as yourself.

Sarvepalli Radhakrishnan, a scholar of comparative religion and philosophy and the second president of India (1962-67), defined Hinduism as 'a fellowship of all who accept the law of right and earnestly seek for the truth'.

> Wars of religion which are the outcome of fanaticism that prompts and justifies the extermination of aliens of different creeds were practically unknown in Hindu India. Of course, here and there were outbursts of fanaticism, but Hinduism as a rule never encouraged persecution for unbelief.
>
> — SARVEPALLI RADHAKRISHNAN,
> *HINDU VIEW OF LIFE* (1960)

Today, the best and most well remembered periods in Indian history are those in which India was at its most confident and tolerant, under the Mauryas, the Guptas, and the Mughals before Aurangzeb—who understood that this was the only way. After all, if Muslims could have felt at home in India, Jinnah would not have insisted on partitioning the country.

Perhaps, after centuries of Mughal and then British rule, Hinduism became insecure and defensive.

But as I hope to have shown, it has really no need to be.

WHAT DO YOU THINK?

These days, most books are bought on Amazon. A book's discoverability is determined by an algorithm, which loves nothing more than a fresh review. The more reviews a book has, the more it gets seen—and bought and read. So it would mean a lot to me if you could take a few seconds to review this book. Even a simple sentence or star rating would be grand.

To keep in touch and hear about new books, subscribe to my very occasional newsletter and receive my recipe for the best mango and saffron lassi.

https://neelburton.kit.com/mangolassi

If you enjoyed this book, you will also enjoy the other books in the Ancient Wisdom series—especially, I think, *The Meaning of Myth* and *The Gang of Three*.